WILLIAM BLAKE
THE MAN

BY
CHARLES GARDNER

AUTHOR OF "VISION AND VESTURE," "THE REDEMPTION OF RELIGION," ETC.

"The men that were with me saw not the vision"
DANIEL

LONDON : J. M. DENT & SONS LIMITED
NEW YORK : E. P. DUTTON & CO.
MCMXIX

THE BURIAL OF MOSES.
Reproduced by kind permission of Mr Sydney Morse.

To

MONICA

PREFACE

THIS book is an attempt to trace the mental and spiritual growth of William Blake as disclosed in his works. After meditating on these for some years an image of the man has risen in my mind. This I have tried to present with the aid of such biographical details as are to be found in Gilchrist's *Life*. My warm thanks are due to Mr and Mrs Sydney Morse for permission to reproduce their beautiful *Prayer of the Infant Jesus*, and *The Burial of Moses*. The photographs were taken by Mr Albert Hester. Also I must thank Mr J. M. Dent for the two designs from an original and invaluable *Job* series in his possession. The rest of the illustrations are from the Print Room of the British Museum.

C. G.

CONTENTS

		PAGE
TITLE-PAGE	. . . .	3
DEDICATION	. . . .	5
PREFACE .	. . . .	7
CONTENTS .	. . . .	9
ILLUSTRATIONS	. . . .	10

CHAPTER

I.	CHILDHOOD AND APPRENTICESHIP	11
II.	COMING OF AGE AND MARRIAGE	21
III.	THE BLUE-STOCKINGS	26
IV.	EARLY MARRIED LIFE AND EARLY WORK . , , ,	37
V.	WESLEY, WHITEFIELD, LAVATER, AND SWEDENBORG . .	46
VI.	THE REBELS	81
VII.	ACTION AND REACTION	102
VIII.	WILLIAM HAYLEY.	114
IX.	THE BIG PROPHETIC BOOKS	131
X.	CROMEK, SIR JOSHUA, STOTHARD, AND CHAUCER . .	153
XI.	THE SUPREME VISION	165
XII.	DECLINING YEARS AND DEATH	169
XIII.	EPILOGUE	189
	INDEX	195

LIST OF ILLUSTRATIONS

THE BURIAL OF MOSES	*Frontispiece*
	FACING PAGE
GLAD DAY	24
LAVATER	50
THE ANCIENT OF DAYS	100
URIZEN IN CHAINS	106
LOS	108
MIRTH AND HER COMPANIONS	124
ALBION	144
THE PRAYER OF THE INFANT JESUS	166
JOB SERIES, DESIGN V	182
JOB SERIES, DESIGN XIV	184
FROM DANTE SERIES	186

WILLIAM BLAKE: THE MAN

CHAPTER I

CHILDHOOD AND APPRENTICESHIP

WILLIAM BLAKE was born on November 28th, 1757, at 28 Broad Street, Carnaby Market, Golden Square.

To-day a large house stands in Broad Street numbered 28, to which is attached a blue disk announcing that William Blake, Poet and Artist, was born there. The house looks old and shabby, and may well have stood a hundred years; but on inquiry one finds that it is a recent erection, and that of Blake's actual house not one stone has been left upon another. One walks through Broad Street and its neighbouring streets hoping to see at least one group of buildings as Blake saw them. But all has changed, and except for a block of houses on one side of Golden Square, there is nothing to remind one of the sharp transitions that a few years can effect. Even the sounds have changed. From the doors and windows of Number 28 is heard day and night the whir of machinery ceaselessly at work to supply the inhabitants of Pall Mall and St James's with electric light. Carnaby Market has vanished, and its glowing colours have reappeared in Berwick Street, where fruits are displayed on public stalls, and where from time to time titled ladies are known to explore in search of a pair of boots, or some other indispensable article of clothing. Great ugly buildings—a brewery, an infirmary given up during the war to Belgian refugees, warehouses—afflict the eye at every turn ; and through the open windows of the upper stories the social regenerator may detect the countless bent backs and expert fingers of tailor hands turning out perfect equipments for noblemen all over the country who come to Regent Street, Maddox Street, and Conduit Street to be measured and fitted and tried.

In Blake's day the transitions in Broad Street were more clearly defined. It had been a fashionable quarter, and still retained a vivid memory of its past glory. The new buildings were shops of a good solid kind, which struck the eye like vivid green paint as they sprang up side by side with the older private houses that time had softened and mellowed.

Blake's father was a hosier. His name was James, he was married to Catherine, and they had five children, William being the second. James was a dissenter, but, like so many dissenters, he liked such important functions as baptism, marriage, and burial to be performed by the Church of England, that there might be no mistake about them. Accordingly, William was taken on December 11th, when he was a fortnight old, to be christened at St James's Church in a Grinling Gibbons font, the highly ornate character of which was fortunately not observed by the tender recipient of baptismal grace.

William was a solitary, imaginative boy. His imagination was first stimulated and nourished by town. His father's home, in sharp contrast with the older houses in the neighbourhood, made him perceive that there was a meaning Past as well as a so-far unmeaning Present : and the moment his imagination escaped into the past it tended to abstraction, but knew no bounds.

Very soon in his solitary walks he found his way into the country, emerging from London on the south side and exploring as far as Peckham Rye, Dulwich, Streatham, and Sydenham. His first glimpse of the country was to him as our first trip abroad to us. The trees, the hills, the grass and the cattle spoke obliquely to an imagination that already had a bias. He loved them—with discretion. To him London was older than the country. Nature has a way of disguising her great age in an ever renewed youthful present. London's present drives one to the past. Nature bewitches her children and will not allow them to transcend her. A great city with its pulsing life carries the exuberant spirit in its mighty rhythm, and yet drives it back to the ancient primeval sources concealed in the eternal kingdom of the imagination. Wordsworth, Nature's lover, soothes and lulls our restlessness and pain, but fails to carry us into the promised land. Blake, the inspired citizen, pierces with his sword through Nature, and will not rest until in England's green and pleasant land he has built Jerusalem, wherein we may feast as comrades and be satisfied with the wine of eternity.

Little William Blake was not like other children, or he might have romped with his three brothers, John, James, and Robert, and his sister, Catherine. But from the first he was peculiar, sensitive, and liable to visions. His first recorded vision was in Peckham Rye. There he saw a tree filled with angels. He was neither startled nor surprised. It seemed entirely natural, and, childlike, he told his vision to his parents when he reached home. Visions were not in his father's line of business. In the dark days of popish supremacy there had been idle monks who thrashed and starved themselves till they saw visions. Even the reformed Church of England knew better than that, and a dissenter of the eighteenth century who spent his spare hours from the shop in reading knew precisely what were the things from which he dissented. He must nip William's visions in the bud, and he would thrash him. Happily, Mrs. Blake stepped between. It was a jarring shock to an over-sensitive child that a heavy penalty awaited the mention of visions. He continued to see them, but he kept them to himself. His brothers and sister were like his father. Robert, who in after years would have understood, was in the middle of his teething, and it did not yet appear what he would be. Hence all things worked together to separate William from his family and to thrust him into the world of imagination.

At this time—he was about nine years old—he became a devourer of books. His mental bias was sufficiently strong to draw to him the books that would nourish him. Percy's *Reliques*, which was sure to be among his father's books, was entirely congenial to him, as later to little Walter Scott. Also Shakespeare and some of the Elizabethans, of whom Ben Jonson was certainly one, were absorbed into his being. Spencer's *Faery Queen* and later poets of his own time—Rowley, Thomson, Chatterton—were his daily companions : and above all he adored with passionate idolatry the then famous *Ossian* of Macpherson.

Swinburne has expressed astonishment that the child Blake could admire such " lank and lamentable counterfeits of the poetical style " as Macpherson supplied to an undiscerning generation. We must remember that in spite of the Highland Society, then meeting in London, Blake had no easy access to the times of Fingal and Ossian, such as we have to-day. There was something in his genius which made him crave for the society of the Celtic heroes and gods. If Macpherson's poetic stream was muddy,

Blake's thirst was too consuming to allow of criticism. What is disconcerting is that the mature Blake should retain his admiration of Macpherson and bracket him with the greatest poets of any age. We can only say that what we have loved with our whole heart in childhood, and has entered for better or worse into the very tissue of our being, we cannot criticize ; and simple, trustful Blake to the end of his days would have reckoned himself guilty of impious disloyalty if he had admitted even to himself that there were spots in his sun.

Blake's reading had effected an invaluable service for him— it peopled his world of imagination. There was terror in his first approach on the threshold, a terror never forgotten and often reproduced in his designs. But when he was pushed beyond the threshold and its covering shadow, he gradually grew accustomed to the changed lights, and he began to discern its forms and its outlines and its colours. These in their turn reacted on the outer world until he saw it not as a hard unsurpassable fact, but a mirror of the inner things which in reality were the substance, the form, and the foundation. Henceforth he valued the forms and outlines of things because they were a sign and pledge to him of the inner resplendent City which was not only built on an eternal foundation but was actually the home of his spirit. As soon as he apprehended the significance of outline he developed an ardent desire to draw.

This impulse was quickly observed by his father and encouraged by him. William was sent to learn drawing from a Mr Pars, who kept a drawing-school in the Strand. Here he copied plaster casts and odd-and-end plaster bits of the human body, the body itself being left severely alone. A certain amount of technical facility was thus acquired, but his education in art advanced more surely from his desultory wanderings in sale-rooms and in the private galleries of munificent noblemen. At the sale-rooms he bought prints often for a few pence, and his little store of prints was added to by gifts from his father, who also presented him with models of the Gladiator, Hercules, Venus of Medici. In this way he gained his first enthusiastic knowledge of Raphael, Michael Angelo, Martin Hemskerck, Albert Dürer and Julio Romano, who were exactly the right teachers for him. Michael Angelo and the Florentine School believed that drawing was the foundation of all great art. Albert Dürer and his great German successors were of the same opinion. William Blake, the little citizen of the heavenly Jerusalem, had known the horror of indefiniteness, and worked through his apprenticeship to joy only when he discovered that the blessed City stood four-square, and was bounded by great walls on its four sides. Hence his selection of prints was instinctive. He knew without being told what helped him to find himself, and he escaped once for all, while still a child, the seductive elegance of his own age.

These were happy years. His mind was already stored with unfashionable knowledge, gleaned chiefly from the robust Elizabethan age, and his spirit, like a mirror, reflected the things he saw with his spiritual eye. His happiness was creative, and he burst into song when he was only eleven in strains that savoured of Ben Jonson, but were wholly fresh and captivating because they were inspired by the first fresh vision of his childhood. There is surely nothing in any language written by a boy of eleven to touch the song: *How sweet I roam'd from field to field.* It is a sudden spring of sparkling water that can never lose its purity.

Blake remained four years with Pars, and then his father, willing that his son should become an artist, apprenticed him in 1771 to Basire in Great Queen Street, Lincoln's Inn Fields.

We who stand far apart from Blake's day can see that this was the best thing that could have happened. Had his father been a rich man, able to pay a heavy premium that his son might be taught by one of the popular engravers of the day, we should have had the distressing picture of Blake moulded different and moulded wrong by a Woollett, a Bartolozzi, or an Angelica Kaufmann, and his whole soul in rebellious and ineffectual protest. As it was, Basire was master of the technical part of his craft, he believed in accurate, definite outline, and not being a man of genius, did not think it necessary that his pupils should turn out servile copies of himself. Blake learnt to handle his tools, to lay a good foundation, and technical proficiency. In after years, when engraving was to be a chief means of expressing his own original vision, he was saved from the painful necessity of having to unlearn much or all of his master's teaching.

After two quiet years with Basire a providential thing happened. Two more apprentices were taken on by him. These were wholly products of the time, and Blake found himself in violent collision with them in aims, methods, and tastes. To keep the peace, Blake was separated from them and sent to draw in Westminster Abbey.

Gothic architecture was as intoxicating a revelation to Blake as the discovery of Michael Angelo and Albert Dürer in the sale-rooms of Christie and Langford. The Chapel of Edward the Confessor, recently piled up with sand-bags to protect it from the desecration of German bombs, became to Blake a little sanctuary. Here his thoughts travelled without fatigue many hundred years

B

back, and the dim background of the Chapel became a fit setting for his bright visions of the past. He copied with silent intensity the monuments of the Confessor, Henry III, Queen Elinor, Philippa, and the beautiful work of Aymer de Valence. These days were decisive for his lifetime. Gothic architecture was germane to his own soul. Its spirit sank inwards and appeared again and again in the architectural fragments of his own designs. There remained for him one more great formative heritage from the past, and then, with his roots well set, he was to reach forward to the future and prophesy in rhythmic words that are meat and drink to us in the twentieth century.

Blake remained with Basire for seven years. During these years he had glimpses of a world different from the one in which his family moved. Oliver Goldsmith, with his fine head, came as a shining messenger, and actually walked into Basire's. Oh ! that he might grow up to have such a head ! Woollett was a visitor, and a sufficiently frequent one to cease to be dazzling even to an overtrustful and enthusiastic apprentice. " One of the most ignorant fellows I ever met," he wrote of him who never at any time could have been congenial to his spirit. Many others appeared there also—silently marked and measured in a way that would have astonished them had they been worthy to know.

Blake's time was not wholly spent in copying the works of others. In his spare hours he threw off songs and designs of his own. These latter were sometimes partly copies of a much-loved master. Thus, *Joseph of Arimathea among the Rocks of Albion* was suggested by Michael Angelo's Crucifixion of St Peter in the Vatican, and the figure of Joseph is a copy.[1] Blake himself

---

[1] This fact was first pointed out by Mr Laurence Binyon.

had written " engraved by W. Blake, 1773, from an old Italian Drawing " ; " Michael Angelo, Pinxit." But already there is more of Blake in this design than of his master. He wrote between the lines, " This is one of the Gothic Artists who built the Cathedrals in what we call the Dark Ages, wandering about in sheep-skins and goat-skins ; of whom the World was not worthy. Such were the Christians in all ages." From which we may gather that Blake was fully conscious that his being a Christian—and his Art was inseparable from his Christianity— had already consigned him to a solitary life in which he might expect persecutions, but certainly not a resting-place.

Blake's apprenticeship with Basire came to a peaceful end in 1778, when he was twenty-one years old. He was now a man, peering forward into a dim and cloudy future, looking backward on a childhood of clearest visions that were already passing, and as it was, according to all precedent, had overstayed their time. One thing was entirely clear—he must earn his own living. Another thing he was conscious of was that he was slowly and surely leaving the past behind. Yet so far, seated amidst the ruins of the Old World, he knew not whither his religious aspirations would lead him. He had fine memories, he had religious and art instincts that refused to be separated, he was finding himself daily in opposition to the admired religionists and artists of his time, and he felt within the strength of immense passion which would surely drive him to the building of the heavenly Jerusalem if he could but get his vision clear again, and know the path which God had before marked out for him to walk in. His vision was to clear after many years. Meanwhile there were tempests and storms to be endured that would reduce still more effectually to wreckage the last remains of the

Old World. That World had spoken with dignity and power through the lips of Dr Johnson, who was himself breaking up and died in 1784. With the death of Johnson the Old World died, to reappear only in a kind of after-mirage ; and young Blake was struggling through the tempestuous years of his passionate youth, turning with pain his eyes from the Past to the Future, and wistfully hoping that the mighty creative power that was already astir in him might fashion a new order in which he and his fellows could live at peace.

CHAPTER II

COMING OF AGE AND MARRIAGE

THE Royal Academy is a British Institution which we all patronize once a year, and then abuse that we may keep our self-respect. We go, impelled by a sense of high duty ; but we presently relax and take our pleasure in Bond Street. In 1778 Bond Street did not lay itself out to encourage revolutionary artists, and Burlington House was not yet finished. The Royal Academy was turned out of Somerset Palace and was still waiting to turn into its new quarters.

Blake, on leaving Basire, immediately joined the Academy and studied in the Antique School under Mr Moser. This was not an auspicious beginning. Moser had scant respect for Michael Angelo and Raphael, while he extolled to the skies the more fleshly works of Le Brun and Rubens. Some of us may wish that Moser had taught Blake to admire Rubens. But an angel from Heaven could not have done that. Clear outline was a necessity to keep him sane ; blurred outline always gave him nightmare. Only the mystic who loves the flesh can rejoice in the roly-poly curves and tints of Rubens' fat Venuses. Moser did his best, and being an old man of seventy-three, felt he might advise a young man in his art studies. But Blake had now known for some years what he really liked, and his impetuosity led him to speak to Moser as if their positions were reversed.

Blake drew at the Academy not only from the antique but from living models. This was distasteful to him, because it was never his aim to reproduce exact portraits of outward things. Always his imagination must pierce through and illumine the object before him, and he found the posed model baffled him in this attempt, and made him scent death rather than life.

These were crowded days for Blake. He could not continue to live under his father's roof in Broad Street without contributing towards the household expenses, and therefore he must do work of marketable value. To this end he received orders for engraving from Johnson and other booksellers. It was drudging work, and Blake was not without his full share of drudgery. To engrave after Stothard was to set a lion to speak in a monstrous little voice. But Stothard had his uses for Blake. Through a fellow-engraver Blake was introduced to Stothard, who, still young, was making a guinea a piece for his contributions to the *Novelist's Magazine*. Broad Street was in the thick of the Artists and Royal Academicians. Once Blake had pierced the magic circle and could meet them on equal terms, instead of merely watching their exits and their entrances through the doors of Broad Street, Poland Street, and Golden Square, they might prove of value to him, not by teaching him to paint as they painted, but by helping him to get customers for his own productions. Stothard had lately made the acquaintance of Flaxman, who had sought him out, and he introduced Blake to Flaxman, who in 1781 took a house at 27 Wardour Street and became Blake's close friend and neighbour.

At this time, in 1780, Blake threw off one of his very own magnificent designs known as *Morning, or Glad Day*. It is the real Blake with only one foot on earth, his head in a flood of light, and the symbols of his grub state—caterpillar and moth—at his feet. The rays of the light are darting north and south and east and west. Blake had weary years before him to work out his salvation to Glad Day. This design makes it certain that he already had had his glimpse of the end, and we shall find that he was not disobedient to the heavenly vision.

London was not without its excitements. Lord George Gordon headed the No-Popery Riots in 1780, and through the unruly violence of the mob, London was in a panic for a week. Lord George was arrested and imprisoned in the Tower, where he was visited by the ubiquitous John Wesley, who found him well instructed in the Bible and not disposed to complain.

It is impossible to trace accurately what books Blake read at this time. It is evident that he observed Wesley and White-field and admired much that he saw in them. But his own religious genius was far removed from theirs, and sought nourishment elsewhere. It is probable that he read Boehme, Paracelsus, Fludd, Madame Guyon, and St Theresa in his spare hours.

But there were other imperious needs surging up in him. The creative passion of love was driving him hither and thither. With his tendency to view all things in the light of eternity, he was passionately in love with the eternal feminine, into which any pair of bright eyes would serve as windows. The particular pair of eyes that captivated him belonged to " a lively little girl " called Polly Wood, with whom he kept company for a while. Polly's conversation was probably no more suitable as a permanent entertainment to Blake than that of a modern flapper. Fortunately, she understood little affairs of the heart much better than he did, not taking them more seriously than they deserved ; and when she saw symptoms of tremendously earnest love-making threatening to engulf her, she quickly shook him off with a sharp stroke, " Are you a fool ? " and left him feeling very lacerated and sorry for himself.

Blake had not long to wait for another manifestation of the eternal feminine. Recovering from an illness at Kew, where he was staying at the house of a market-gardener named Boucher, he told his grief to the gardener's daughter Catherine, who declared that she pitied him from the heart. There was the authentic voice of the eternal feminine. " Do you pity me ? " he gasped. " Yes ! I do most sincerely " the voice continued. " Then I love you ! " and his fate was sealed. William Blake and Catherine Boucher were married quietly at St Mary's Church, Battersea, on August 18th, 1782, and the happy pair, leaving their parental nests, made their first little home together in lodgings at 23 Green Street, Leicester Fields.

Blake's worldly goods with all of which he endowed his bride were not plentiful. A portfolio of prints which had been growing in bulk during fifteen years was his darling treasure. Money he had none. But he had immense capacity for sustained application and work. His engravings made small but sure returns, and for the last four years he had turned his attention to watercolour, and in 1780 had even exhibited in the Royal Academy. And he was making friends. Friend Flaxman lived near in Wardour Street, friend Fuseli in Broad Street. Stothard was kind. A young man with sanguine temperament like Blake might expect anything to turn up.

His wife brought no gold with her ; but she brought a faithful maternal heart, unlimited faith in her husband, a teachable spirit, and a willingness to turn her hand to all that was necessary to make and keep a little home for the man-child of her heart.

GLAD DAY.

She had made her mark in the marriage register of St Mary's Church.   A woman with such endowments, unspoilt by education, was virgin soil that would yield whatever her husband willed. It was no long time before she learnt of him to write, draw, and engrave, all of which acquirements she placed in perfect loyalty at his disposal.

We have seen that Blake's circle of acquaintances widened much from the day he became a student at the Royal Academy. But artists are not necessarily in Society, and if one can believe what everyone says they are apt to be bohemian.   Now that Blake was a married man, he could not be indifferent to the grades of the social ladder ; and when Flaxman introduced him to the elegant and cultured Mrs Mathew at 27 Rathbone Place, he not only had hopes of a useful patron for himself, but also that the accomplished lady might be a kind friend to his wife.   She had been truly kind to Flaxman for many years, and it is reasonable to suppose that while benefiting him she had herself benefited by his pure classicism and romanticism combined.   Thus equipped, she needed only to extend her sympathies towards mysticism, and then she might include even Blake himself among her good works.   But she and her sister Blue-stockings deserve a chapter to themselves.

CHAPTER III

THE BLUE-STOCKINGS

POSTERITY is spiteful towards those who do not make good their claim to immortality ; and for a long time the Blue-stockings have been the butt of the superior modern. Yet they were remarkable women, and by their dash to capture for themselves some of the treasures of man's learning they helped to open up a new way for the modern woman.

We can dispense no doubt with Mrs Montagu's *Essay*, in which she defends Shakespeare against the rash onslaught of Voltaire. We may even forget her three *Dialogues of the Dead*, although Mrs Modish speaks with the genuine accent of the polite world : " Indeed, Mr Mercury, I cannot have the pleasure of waiting upon you now, I am engaged, absolutely engaged." (There was a fourth Dialogue returned to her by Lord Lyttelton in which Cleopatra tells Berenice only what every woman knows.) But we cannot forgo without loss to ourselves her letters to the Duchess of Portland and many other friends, which are lively, witty, and entertaining, and second in her time only to those of that prince of letter-writers, Horace Walpole.

Mrs Montagu's friends did their best to turn her head. Mrs Carter writes to her of " the elegant brilliancy of my dearest Mrs Montagu," and not content with prose as a medium of praise, sends her an ode which leads up by a strong crescendo to these two verses :

" O blest with ev'ry talent, ev'ry Grace
Which native Fire, or happy Art supplies,
How short a Period, how confined a Space,
Must bound thy shining Course below the Skies !

For wider Glories, for immortal Fame,
Were all those talents, all those Graces given :
And may thy life pursue that noblest aim,
The final plaudit of approving Heav'n."

Mrs Carter thought that Dr Johnson's preface to Shakespeare was " very defective," and she adds to Mrs Montagu, certain that her Latin will be understood without the aid of a dictionary : " Res integra tibi reservatur." Elsewhere she writes : " you, who have proved yourself the most accurate and judicious of all his commentators." This opinion was shared by the entire circle of Blue-stockings, and even outside that charmed circle the Reverend Montagu Pennington, nephew of Mrs Carter and godson of Mrs Montagu, felt that she was guilty of something like mortal sin in omitting to defend the British Public against the pernicious influence of Lord Chesterfield's *Letters to his Son*.

Mrs Carter, loaded with languages, and much addicted to snuff and green tea, was scarcely inferior to Mrs Montagu. She was modest and almost apologetic for her much learning. She and the rest of the heady sisterhood were not without misgivings that in pursuing man's studies they might become manly, and therefore they never ceased to express in season and out of season pious female sentiments. Indeed, Mrs Carter protested against being thought of as a walking tripod, and was what used to be called " a sweet woman." Thus she writes of " the infernal composition of deadly weeds made up by Voltaire." *Candide* was " so horrid in all respects." *Werther* she detested. She is relieved to hear that Pascal is " very respectable," for she considered him " a dangerous author to all kinds of readers." Rousseau " quite sunk her spirits." Of course her spirits were liable to the same shock during her extensive readings among the ancients, and, indeed, she said that Quintilian's impiety was " quite shocking "; but very justly she considered that they were to be excused because they had not the light of revelation, while Voltaire and Rousseau were sinning against that light.

Mrs Carter and Mrs Montagu fully agreed in their admiration for Mrs Vesey, whom they familiarly called " our Sylph." Hannah More in her *Bas Bleu* seems to reckon her the first of the Blues, and specially commends her for the skill she displayed in breaking the formidable circle that Mrs Montagu's guests were forced to make. Her lively Irish nature was refreshing to Mrs Carter, her head full and aching after a strenuous tussle with Aristotle's *Ethics*. She wrote to Mrs Montagu : " As little of the turbulent as there is in her (our Sylph's) composition, the uproar of a mighty sea is as much adapted to the sublime of her imagination, as the soft murmurs of a gliding stream to the gentleness of her temper."

The conversaziones of the Blue-stockings were as successful as might be. There was always a difficulty in procuring men. Dr Johnson could be baited from time to time. Horace Walpole, driven by curiosity, appeared and disappeared. At Mrs Ord's, 35 Queen Anne Street, where Fanny Burney met " everything delectable in the Blue way," one catches a glimpse of Mr

Smelt, Captain Phillips, Dr Burney, Lord Mulgrave, Sir Lucas Pepys, and the Bishop of London. The kindness and patronage of Lord Bath and Lord Lyttelton could always be relied upon. Yet there was no full and easy interchange of ideas with men. The time had not yet come. In France it had been accomplished by the ladies who were willing to step beyond the bounds of strict propriety, but the pious English Blues were the last to wish to follow the example of their French sisters. And so their best chance of getting a man was to catch one young and struggling whom they might patronize and be kind to.

In this way all the luck fell to Mrs Mathew, of 27 Rathbone Place. If Mrs Montagu had the advantage of a rich and indulgent husband, Mrs Mathew excelled all in the respectability of hers. The Reverend Henry Mathew was incumbent of Percy Chapel, Charlotte Street, and afternoon preacher at St Martin's-in-the-Fields. The latter church alone is sufficient to make a man's reputation ; but Mr Mathew had already made his both by his piety and his taste.

No one has such opportunities as one of the priesthood for discovering promising young men. Mr Mathew's first find was little Flaxman struggling with a Latin book. Learning the nature of the book, he promised him a better and invited him to his house. Mrs Mathew herself was well read in Latin and Greek, and here was a boy of genius thrown into her very lap. Rising to the great occasion, she taught him, read to him while he sketched, and by her treatment of him alone made more than amends for being a Blue.

When Flaxman was full grown he did all in his power to show his gratitude. Mrs Mathew was desirous to turn her back parlour into a Gothic chamber. Here was an opportunity. Flaxman modelled little figures of sand and putty and placed them in niches. Another protégé, Oram, son of old Oram and Loutherbourg's assistant, painted the windows, and between them they made the book-cases, tables, and chairs to match. With such a room, Mrs Mathew might ask whom she would and not be ashamed. To her tea parties came Mrs Montagu, Mrs Carter when staying in Clarges Street, Mrs Barbauld, Mrs Chapone, Mrs Brooke, and many others.

Blake and Flaxman first met in 1780 and soon became friends. Flaxman, by native bent and Mrs Mathew's teaching, was steeped in Greek. By this time he had shown himself wonderful alike in his designs and sculptures, and already held a high place in what has been called the Second Renaissance.

Blake was a romantic rather than a Greek, but as a later Greek, Goethe, has assured us that there is no antagonism between a true romantic and a true Greek, it is not surprising that the two men found a deep congeniality of spirit. There was an even deeper fellowship, which became explicit later on when both concurred in admiring Swedenborg.

Flaxman, generously anxious that his friend should get on, introduced him, in 1782, to Mr and Mrs Mathew, who asked him and Mrs Blake to their evenings. And so at last we see rebel Blake and his illiterate wife in the midst of a charmed circle of Blues who were mistresses of everything that was learned, cultured, elegant, decorous, and *du bon ton*.

Our first glimpse of Blake in Society we owe to John Thomas Smith, Keeper of the Prints at the British Museum and frequent visitor at Mrs Mathew's. He says in his *Book for a Rainy Day* : " At Mrs Mathew's most agreeable conversaziones I first met the late William Blake, the artist, to whom she and Mr Flaxman had been truly kind. There I have often heard him read and sing several of his poems. He was listened to by the company with profound silence, and allowed by most of the visitors to possess original and extraordinary merit."

That is a pleasant picture. Would that we had been there ! But as time went on several things became clear to Blake and likewise to the company, only their interpretation of the situation differed. Mrs Blake proved a touchstone to the other ladies. They of course could see at once that she was not a lady, but that they must be kind to her. She, not having read Mrs Chapone on the improvement of the mind or practised the elegancies, was quite unable to imitate their manners and catch their tone. She was throughout a simple, direct, noble woman set down in the midst of an artificial society, and she was made to suffer accordingly. These things sank deep into Blake, to reappear again as poems in his *Ideas of Good and Evil.* Many times he himself felt the same discomfort both at Mrs Mathew's and later at Mr Hayley's. The words he puts into Mary's (Catherine's) lips he speaks in his own person in lines that he afterwards addressed to Flaxman :

> " Oh, why was I born with a different face ?
> Why was I not born like this envious race ?
> Why did Heaven adorn me with bountiful hand,
> And then set me down in an envious land ? "

Still Blake was " allowed by most of the visitors to possess original and extraordinary merit." The songs he sang were inspired by his reading of the Elizabethans, whom the Blues could appreciate. The *Poetical Sketches* came within the purview of professed admirers of Ben Jonson and Spenser ; and therefore

Mrs Mathew could genuinely agree with Flaxman that it was worth helping Blake to get them published. The *Poetical Sketches* were gathered together and printed at the expense of Flaxman and the Mathews, Mr Mathew himself writing an apologetic *Advertisement* which would save his skin and lack of discernment if the pieces were unapproved by the great Public. Since it is short, I will quote it entire :

" The following sketches were the production of untutored youth, commenced in his twelfth, and occasionally resumed by the author till his twentieth year ; since which time, his talents having been wholly directed to the attainment of excellence in his profession, he has been deprived of the leisure requisite to such a revisal of these sheets as might have rendered them less unfit to meet the public eye. Conscious of the irregularities and defects to be found in almost every page, his friends have still believed that they possessed a poetical originality, which merited some respite from oblivion. These their opinions remain, however, to be now reproved or confirmed by a less partial public."

It was hardly want of leisure that had prevented Blake from polishing his verses. Mr Mathew had argued with him on the necessity, and he had proved tiresomely obstinate, and, what is worse, remained of the same opinion eight years afterwards when he wrote in *The Marriage of Heaven and Hell* : " Improvement makes strait roads, but the crooked roads without Improvement are roads of Genius."

Mr Mathew was but one of those Bunglers that " can never see perfection, but in the journeyman's labour." However, he saved his name for his generation and lost it for posterity.

Blake's *Poetical Sketches* were printed but not published. The copies were handed over to him to give or sell, but they brought him neither fame nor money.

It is long since anyone doubted the worth of the *Poetical Sketches*. The twentieth century wholly endorses the glowing and just criticism that Swinburne wrote fifty years ago. It must have startled the stolid bookish people of the 'sixties to be told that the best of Blake's *Poetical Sketches—To Spring, To Memory, To the Muses, To the Evening Star*—were comparable to the world's best in any age. Swinburne frequently exaggerated in his excitement ; but here was no exaggeration, and the poems which were once thought by a partial friend " to merit some respite from oblivion " are now reckoned among the chief pearls of great price in England's rich treasury of Songs.

There remains little more for the critic to say, but the biographer turns to these *Sketches* for any intimation of Blake's spiritual and mental growth.

We must not be misled by the " scent and sound of Elizabethan times " that is upon them. It is of course interesting to the literary mind to discover Ben Jonson in *How sweet I roamed*, Beaumont and Fletcher in *My Silks and fine Array*, Webster in the *Mad Song*, and Shakespeare in *King Edward the Third* ; but these intimations of kinship are only such as are found in original geniuses of the same age. That which gives life and immortality and irresistible sweetness to the songs is Blake's own child-spirit seeing with wide-eyed simplicity the simple commonplace things of this world that God made, and that are to the pure in heart the immediate revelation of Him. If in fashioning into Song the things that he saw Blake refuses the artifice of his time and catches the scent and sound of a more robust age, yet the prime

c

inspiration was entirely his own ; and we can only wonder that such inspiration should have come to him while still a mere boy.

The other pieces in the collection, though of much less importance, have their interest. *Fair Elinor* with the " silent tower," the " castle gate," the " dreary vaults," and " sickly smells," like Horace Walpole's *Mysterious Mother* and *Castle of Otranto*, is not of the time but anticipatory of the romantic horrors that Mrs Radcliffe was to make entirely her own. *Gwen King of Norway* and *King Edward the Third* are remarkable for their martial language. This was no accident. Blake was a born fighter. The heroic side of War stirred his spirit, even though

> " The God of War is drunk with blood ;
> The Earth doth faint and fail :
> The stench of blood makes sick the Heav'ns ;
> Ghosts glut the throat of Hell ! "

His feeling for England recalls old John of Gaunt's speech :

> " Lord Percy cannot mean that we should suffer
> This disgrace : if so, we are not sovereigns
> Of the sea—our right, that Heaven gave
> To England, when at the birth of nature
> She was seated in the deep ; the Ocean ceas'd
> His mighty roar, and fawning play'd around
> Her snowy feet, and own'd his awful Queen."

Grim War is a means to glorious liberty :

> " Then let the clarion of War begin ;
> I'll fight and weep, 'tis in my country's cause ;
> I'll weep and shout for glorious liberty.
> Grim War shall laugh and shout, decked in tears,

And blood shall flow like streams across the meadows,
That murmur down their pebbly channels, and
Spend their sweet lives to do their country service :
Then shall England's verdure shoot, her fields shall smile,
Her ships shall sing across the foaming sea,
Her mariners shall use the flute and viol,
And rattling guns, and black and dreary war,
Shall be no more."

Later on the War spirit in him, without diminishing, underwent a change. It is still England's green and pleasant fields that he loves, and he still longs for glorious liberty. This shall be effected by the building of Jerusalem. But as the root of the evil is in man, the weapons of his warfare become spiritual. Casting aside the rattling guns, he shouts :

" Bring me my bow of burning gold,
Bring me my arrows of desire ;
Bring me my spear ; O clouds unfold !
Bring me my chariot of fire !

I will not cease from mental fight
Nor shall my sword sleep in my hand,
Till we have built Jerusalem
In England's green and pleasant land."

For War breeds hate and every evil thing. Until we arouse ourselves and fight like warriors the evil that is in ourselves, there can be no glorious liberty, whether for England or any other nation of the world.

The *Poetical Sketches* were a failure. Mrs Mathew had generously tried to help, but her influence was not wide.

A magnificent opportunity had come to the Blue-stockings, and to Mrs Montagu in particular, who with all her money and wide influence, which she was always ready to use for her needy friends, might have helped quite incalculably when Blake most needed it, and earned our undying gratitude. Yet we must be just and not blame them for their lost opportunity. Their significance lies in the fact that they objected to being perfect dunces like the rest of their English sisters, and so they made a bold dash to understand the things that men understand. They were not the first learned women the world had seen. The ladies of the Italian Renaissance could have given them points all round. Their work was that of restoration and not revolution, and that was more than sufficient to occupy their thoughts and energies without their peering into the new world that was at work in Blake. When whiffs of the new spirit blew on them from Voltaire, Rousseau, Goethe, and Hume, they were chilled and shocked, and thanked Heaven that in Dr Johnson there was a champion who knew all about the new and stoutly maintained the old. That was sufficient for them. Unfortunately they lived at a time when Society was more than usually artificial and woman suppressed, and the odd contrast between them and their sisters made them appear to men somewhat as monsters, like singing mice or performing pigs. The charge of being a Blue-stocking must always brand with a stigma, but happily now that women are establishing their right to meet men on an equality, the charge need never be made again.

CHAPTER IV

EARLY MARRIED LIFE AND EARLY WORK

WE saw that William and Catherine Blake after their marriage settled at 23 Green Street, Leicester Fields. This was in 1782. Here they remained for two years, learning, not without pain, to adjust themselves to each other. Mrs Blake's love was maternal and whole-hearted. Hers was not a nature to question why love should involve the accepting of immeasurable cares. The cares came one by one and not always singly, and she meekly and bravely accepted them, contented to live her life in her husband's life, and happy when she perceived that she could smooth his path and shelter him from rough blasts.

Blake at this time was an extraordinarily difficult man to live with. He was by turns vehement, passionate, wildly self-assertive, and submissive to others far inferior to himself. His visions were less bright than they had been, and his mind was choked with theories about the elemental things of life that every woman understands by instinct. He was conscious of his own genius and of the shortcomings of his successful contemporaries. His rampant egotism sowed his consciousness with resentments that poisoned his blood and bred bitterness. He made frantic efforts to grasp the liberty he had seen from afar, but he only succeeded in confounding liberty with licence, and peremptorily demanding the latter with his wife in a way that was bound to give her pain.

I will not attempt to lift further the veil of their early married life. We have no right to pry. Mr Ellis has constructed this period as far as is possible from the poems of Blake, and to his *Real Blake* I must refer the curious reader; but for my own part I am content to note the signs of trouble in the various poems and not to probe deeper into the secret things which no right-minded person can ever wish to be proclaimed on the house-top. Suffice it to say that Mrs Blake's self-forgetful love won the day, and when the early storms had passed, and the adjustments been made, they were united by a bond which, untouched by the fickleness of the flesh, could defy all shocks and changes because it was founded on the enduring reality of the spirit.

In the early years of married life Blake continued with his wife's company the long walks which had been an early habit. Nothing could have been better for him. Walking till he was tired, rhythmic swing of his arms, unchecked sweating, did more than all else to cleanse his whole being and to cause that uprise of the spirit which was eventually to bring unity and peace to his chaotic and divided self.

His marriage had disturbed another elemental relationship of life. His father disapproved of it, and this led to an estrangement. We must admit that the father had not acquitted himself badly of his paternal duties. It is true he had foolishly wished to thrash him for reporting his visions, believing that the boy lied; but he had helped him to be an artist, and had never really opposed him when a boy. No one can reasonably demand more of a father. Nature has no superstitions about parent birds when their young have left the home nest. Gratitude and reverence to parents is still a beautiful thing, and would doubtless be given spontaneously to them if they could learn not to interfere when their children have grown up.

It has often been affirmed that the old man was a student of Swedenborg. If so, there had been at once a bond of sympathy between father and son. But the truth is that he had not read much of Swedenborg for the simple reason that he died four years before any theological work of importance by Swedenborg was translated into English. Everything shows that the father could not understand the son, who must have appeared to him eccentric, headlong, and obstinate. When William heard on July 4th, 1784, of his father's death, he paid all due respect to his memory, but he was not moved by any violent grief.

We do not suppose that Mr Blake made his fortune by hosiery, but he left a little money which was divided among the sons. James took on the business and the mother lived with him. William, assisted by Mrs Mathew (if we may trust the testimony of J. T. Smith), took the house Number 27, next door to his brother, and there he opened a print shop in partnership with Parker, who had been a fellow-pupil at Basire's. Robert, who was teething when we last saw him, was now grown up and proved understanding and sympathetic of William's visionary point of view. It was agreed that Robert should live with William at Number 27 and become his apprentice.

Once more Blake was all mixed up with his immediate kith and kin. When one remembers that he had no illusions about fathers and saw clearly that the father of one's flesh might be the enemy of one's spirit, it seems incredible that he should have planted himself and his wife next door to a brother who was, he knew, an enemy to his spirit, and to a mother who would hardly approve of the young wife, and who would not be behindhand with her advice ; but Blake was not strong in common sense, nor could he keep his neck out of a noose until it had first nearly strangled him.

Robert was a comfort to him, but he can only have added to Mrs Blake's cares. For at this time William was passionately devoted to Robert, and his feeling to his wife had not yet quite resolved itself into that enduring comradeship which was to be his priceless treasure to the end of his days. The oft-repeated tale of Mrs Blake's obedience when her husband said peremptorily : "Kneel down and beg Robert's pardon directly, or you will never see my face again," throws a searchlight on the whole situation. One sees William's peril and Catherine's care, and how her self-forgetful love was the one thing that could bring these discordant elements into a lasting harmony.

This arrangement lasted for two and a half years, when Robert fell desperately ill. William nursed him tenderly, and during the last fortnight sat with him day and night. At the end he saw Robert's soul rise from his body, clapping its hands for joy as it ascended to its perfect life of liberty. Then William, tired out, went to sleep, and did not wake up till after three days and three nights.

The print shop was not successful. Blake lacked the necessary business quality, and the failure was aggravated by disagreements with Parker. The partnership was dissolved, Parker going his own way, and engraving chiefly after Stothard, and Blake closing the shop and retiring with his wife to the other end of Poland Street, which joins Broad Street with Oxford Street. There at Number 28 (now pulled down and replaced) the two, having lost everything, set about in a nearer fellowship to retrieve their fortunes and face the unknown future with as much courage as might be.

Here it is necessary to review briefly Blake's works in engraving and design. We have seen that his instinct when a boy led him directly to the Masters of the Past who could guide him best until he came to himself. The greatest of these were Michael Angelo and Albert Dürer. He did not at first study these demigods and then adopt their principles. He formulated his principles from his immediate experience of Reality, and then rejoiced to find that the men he worshipped produced splendid examples of his principles. First among these was the value of outline. His spiritual eye being opened at a very early age, it was always self-evident to him that the outer world was a vegetable mirror of the inner, and corresponded with it even in the minutest details. If he saw in the outer colour and form, he immediately looked at the inner for the reality of both ; and to his inexpressible joy he not only found what he sought, but also that they so far transcended the outer things that he who saw only the outer could have only the dimmest idea of the wondrous beauty and glory of the archetypes. Hence, with his eye on the eternal outline, he declared consistently all his life that the essence of a body is in its form, and that no man can be a great artist who does not build up his art on the foundation of good drawing. Oil as a medium blurred the outline, and therefore he preferred to work in water-colour. But engraving even better than water-colour, enabled him to apply his principle. It was simply incredible to him that any engraver could undervalue drawing. If engraving lost drawing, it lost all character and expression, and therefore his indignation was aroused with the Woolletts and Bartolozzis, who in this respect were mortal sinners. We can see that such a principle was a necessity for Blake with his peculiar mind, and was even a safeguard to its sanity ; but we have a perfect right to observe that whatever obscures the outlines of things, as twilight, also removes the barriers that hinder our approach to the unseen, and therefore we may enunciate another principle, that one property of a body is its contribution to atmosphere, with its power to evoke our subjective selves. Holding this as a correlative to Blake's axiom, we can do full justice no only to Michael Angelo, Albert Dürer, Raphael, and Blake, but also to Titian, Rubens, and Rembrandt, whom Blake despised. Unfortunately, Blake held to his principle so rigidly that it was apt to lead him into false admirations. We have seen how unduly he admired Macpherson, and here we have to note further that whomsoever of his contemporaries drew the human figure correctly he immediately extolled to the skies, and always with oblique reference of disdain to others whom we have come to think were intrinsically better artists. Hence he admired Mortimer, whom we just remember as the illustrator of Fanny Burney's *Evelina*, whose substantial immortality gives him vicarious and ghostly existence. He also admired Hamilton. In the violent alternations of his mood we have seen how submissive and meek he could be. In such a mood he allowed Mortimer and Hamilton to influence him to such a degree that he actually distrusted the genius in himself which could inspire *Glad Day*, and produced such lifeless imitations of Mortimer's historical style as the *Penance of Jane Shore* (1778), *King Edward and Queen Elinor* (1780), and *Earl Godwin* (1780).

Blake's deferences were not always thus unfortunate. He appreciated Hogarth for his intrinsic value at a time when respectable people patronized him for pictured moralities. We cannot imagine a greater contrast than Blake the frugal seer and Hogarth " the typical carnivorous Englishman." Outline was their meeting-ground. Hogarth saw, we may say detected, in the scenes that marked the progresses of the Rake and the Harlot, a full pulsing life and an unexpected beauty. When he would express what he saw, with a mighty stretch he shook off all foreign influences and set about to express himself naturally and in his own way. His hand appropriated to its use the power of the line, more particularly the vitality of the curved line, with the amazing result that the moment we forget his " moralities," we see in him an exuberant artist of the beautiful. Blake was wholly with him in all this. We rejoice for the seeing eye that Blake and Hogarth cast on the shady side of life, but our wonder and amazement pass into worship when we perceive that this was included in the vision of Him who was called in derision the Friend of Publicans and Sinners, but was contented to speak of Himself as the Son of Man.

Blake affirmed that Hogarth's execution could not be copied or improved. He borrowed from his *Satan, Sin and Death at Hell's Gate*, which is hardly one of Hogarth's masterpieces, for a water-colour of the same subject, and he engraved, after Hogarth, *When my Hero in Court Appears* in the Beggar's Opera (1790).

Blake produced two water-colours in 1784 which show that his thoughts on war were already undergoing a change. These are *War unchained by an Angel—Fire, Pestilence and Famine following*, and *A Breach in a City—the Morning after a Battle*.

Blake had been watching closely the course of affairs on the other side of the Atlantic. While men's minds were becoming more and more inflamed with the thought of war, he was criticizing it with the searching rays of his spiritual vision and finding himself compelled to revise his ideas, which he had taken without question from Shakespeare, and had expressed in the *Poetical Sketches*.   Then, in spite of seas of blood, he glorified war ; now, as he began to consider the abominations that it lets loose on overburdened mankind—Fire, Pestilence and Famine— he included it in the abominations as a thing altogether useless and despicable.   He felt a peculiar joy when peace was this year signed with the North American States.

During these years (1773–84) Blake accomplished an immense amount of engraving, chiefly after Stothard.   These engravings must come as a surprise to those who only know his own sublime designs, that reveal might, power, terror, and immense energy, and not the softer things that we associate with grace. It is sufficient to mention those plates that Blake engraved after Stothard in Ritson's *English Songs* to show that he, like Michael Angelo and Milton, could do not only the works that call for massive power, but also the graceful and lovely things that can be done by genius not quite so rare.   But I must leave the consideration of Blake's relation, personal and artistic, to Stothard to a later chapter, when I come to speak about the *Canterbury Pilgrims*.

Blake's songs, poems, and designs came to birth side by side. Where the engravings were not after his own designs, but after other artists, he knew exactly what to do with them.   But sooner or later, as his own productions of wedded poem and design grew under his hands, the anxious question of publication arose, and by this time it was perplexingly clear to him that his spiritual productions were not for every taste, and that it would be difficult to find anyone who would run the risk of being his publisher.   His *Poetical Sketches* were printed, though not published, through the kindness of Mrs Mathew, but there was no likelihood that any of the Blue-stockings would be kind in a helpful way to him again.

While pondering this difficulty day and night, and increasingly urged by poverty, his brother Robert came to him and directed him what he was to do. He told him to write his poems and designs on copper with an ineffaceable liquid, and with aquafortis to eat away the remainder of the plate until the writing and designs were left in clear relief. Then he might take as many copies as he liked, and just touch them up by hand.

According to Gilchrist, Mr and Mrs Blake possessed just half-a-crown, with which Mrs Blake went out and bought the necessary materials, returning with eightpence change in her pocket. At once they set to work, the wife proving an apt pupil, and thus, with the exception of *The French Revolution*, Blake engraved and published his own creations, experiencing the rare joy of being at once both the creator and the handicrafts-man of his works.

Robert visited William continually to the end of his life, bringing him consolation and encouragement during times of anxiety and stress.

These supernatural happenings in the life of Blake read as simply and naturally as the beautiful stories of St Francis converting brother Wolf or receiving the sacred stigmata. There was nothing of the modern spiritualist's paraphernalia—no medium, no trance, no tappings. Blake was born with his inner spiritual eye open, his outer bodily eye, contrary to general custom, proving sluggish. Hence he was able to keep a natural simplicity amidst things which are too apt to stir only the thaumaturgic appetite of other people.

CHAPTER V

WESLEY, WHITEFIELD, LAVATER, AND SWEDENBORG

BLAKE's manifold nature lacked, so far, a co-ordinating principle. From his earliest years religion had been a reality to him, and so had art, music, literature, but not one of these was so dominant over the rest as to make them subservient. Each lived its separate life and was likely to continue to do so, unless his religion could become forceful and definite enough to penetrate the others and bind them into a higher unity.

His religion had been fed by vision. His visions came to him so naturally that it never occurred to him that others might regard them as symptoms of abnormality or insanity. The thrashing that his father gave him when he told at home what he had seen at Peckham Rye was a memorable occasion, like conversion to some people, only it opened his outer eye and not his inner.

The visions made several things clear to his understanding. He early distinguished between inner and outer vision, supernatural and natural religion. Religion was never a matter of opinion, always of experience. Christ's language was also his own, "We speak that we do know, and testify that we have seen." He felt the same mild surprise at hearing religion denied as he would at the denial of the sun by a blind man. But the reason of such blindness was also quite clear to him. Spiritual things are spiritually discerned. The spiritual man sought no other evidence than

46

that of his spiritual discernment. If the natural man were ever to arrive at spiritual vision, it must be by a new birth of the Spirit. Thus Blake knew from the beginning the inward meaning of Christ's words to Nicodemus, " Verily, verily, I say unto you, Except a man be born again, he cannot see the Kingdom of Heaven. . . . That which is born of the flesh is flesh, that which is born of the Spirit is spirit." Blake was never in danger at any time in his life of becoming enmeshed in natural religion. His escape was more instinctive if less effectual than that of his philosophical contemporary who sought to combat his difficulties by working out an elaborate analogy between natural and revealed religion.

The man who knows by experience what it is to be born again knows also how clamorous the new life within is for nourishment. Blake was driven to the mystics for food. We know by his repeated references in his long poems that St Theresa, Madame Guyon, Paracelsus and Jacob Boehme fed his supersensual life. But besides appealing to the past, he looked around to listen to what his contemporaries had to say to him. It is evident that he would listen only to those who were as clear as himself on the experience of the new birth.

It is not surprising that the high church divines of the eighteenth century had little to say for him. They were more eager to show to the leaders of the enthusiastic methodist party that regeneration took place in Holy Baptism than to make sure that they had exhausted its meaning in their experience. Their views might be extremely correct ; but anything more dull and uninspiring than their sermons and collected works could hardly be found. Blake had no need to examine them particularly, for the best high churchman of the time was Dr Johnson, and he already had his eye on him.

Dr Johnson to the end was a particular kind of grand school-master. He believed in the Christian revelation fervently, and he believed, also with fervour, in the rod, in Latin, in scholarship, and in the drastic repression of the young. He who declared that he would never disgrace the walls of the Abbey by writing for it an epitaph in English, could hardly have seen anything worth his notice in the ignorant Blake and his still more ignorant wife ; and Blake in his turn, unnoticed and unknown, living a severely abstemious life, was too apt to ruminate on Johnson's gluttony and pension, and to conclude that the latter was a reward for barren learning.

It is as well that Johnson and Blake never met. Neither could have worked through his prejudices. They lived in a different world, and moved from a different centre. Johnson viewed the wreckage of the Old World, and then with undaunted courage and indomitable will set himself to build out of the wreckage a covering for himself and his friends. Blake, conscious that dawn was stirring on the wreckage of the dark night, was straining his vision to catch the outline of the new emerging world. Johnson's was a superb mind working within too narrow bounds. Blake's was so far the promise of an unimagined type. We who look backward over the lapse of a hundred years can reverence both men, but it is Blake who is the more inspiring and fruitful.

One other high church divine, William Law, Blake should have read, but strangely makes no mention of. Law's *Serious Call to a Devout and Holy Life* and his *Christian Perfection* were more likely to appeal to Johnson than to Blake, but the later books, *The Spirit of Prayer* and *The Spirit of Love*, written after he had come under the influence of Boehme, while estranging him from Johnson and Wesley, might have brought him and

Blake face to face. Both books are more beautiful than anything written by Wesley, Whitefield, or Swedenborg. Perhaps, as Blake already had read something of Boehme, he found that Law had nothing to add to his knowledge.

There is ample evidence that Blake turned his full attention on to Wesley, Whitefield, and Hervey, and watched them with sympathy. These men were proclaiming everywhere the need of being born again. No one met Blake so definitely on what he had always seen clearly, with large, childlike vision. When Samuel Foote, representative of a thousand others, carelessly threw the epithet "hypocrite" at Whitefield's head, Blake was indignant, and accurately designated the actor as the hypocrite. With perfect justice he pointed out that if Whitefield confessed his sins before all the world, and never pretended to be free from the passions that burn in other men, he was certainly an honest and sincere man. To pounce on a Christian who inadvertently falls, and call him a hypocrite, is as usual now as in Blake's day, but it comes with astonishing gracelessness from the lips of those who have spent their youthful passions in wanton waste, and, wearied and bored, are bidding for a respectable middle age.

Whitefield had pungent things to say to respectable moralists. He had no milder term than " filthy rags " for their dull moralities. If he sought to cover his nakedness with the garment of Christ's righteousness, Blake, while using a different phrase, perfectly understood him and sympathized. But then came the divergence. Whitefield's doctrine of the new birth was inextricably bound up with crude doctrines of Christ's substitutionary death and imputed righteousness, and Blake, who had experienced the new birth quite apart from faith in these particular Calvinist dogmas, felt no need to cling to what his instinctive feeling rejected ; and,

D

what with him was final, he found that Whitefield not only left his æsthetic faculties starved, but actually believed that as the arts came from Tubal and Tubal-cain, and they were descended from Cain, who had been cursed, they must necessarily have their origin from hell.

Hervey carried Blake as far as Whitefield, and no farther. Some years later, when Blake had diverged widely from Whitefield and Hervey, he still remembered them with tenderness and affection ; and placing them with Fénelon, Madame Guyon, St Theresa (an odd assortment !), saw them at Los' South Gate, " with all the gentle souls who guide the great Wine-press of Love." [1]

Blake found that he could keep company with Wesley for a longer time. Wesley had no rigid Calvinism, and he was not content unless imputed righteousness should pass by a second blessing into imparted holiness. Here also Blake's language was wholly different from Wesley's, but the thing he arrived at— the unification of all his powers under the inspiration and creative force of his imagination—led him along a path very like that trodden by Wesley and his methodists as they pressed towards the goal of entire sanctification. It is important to go behind words to things, but it is equally important to come back to a form of sound words. The methodists have been imprisoned by their wordy formulæ, while Blake by his vision of the things behind words not only preserved his freedom, but also, by freeing his imagination, was enabled to create beautiful rhythmic words which invoke instead of imprison.

Among his contemporaries Blake discovered a deeper kinship with Lavater than with any of these. Whitefield and Wesley

[1] *Jerusalem*, 72. 50–52.

JOHN GASPAR LAVATER.
Engraved by Blake.

had succeeded in reviving in themselves the first glow and enthusiasm of protestantism. Lavater is once removed from his zealous protestant forefathers, and the things that they had repressed were making their reappearance in him. Among these was the feeling for the beautiful, which, as he welcomed and nourished it, deepened his sympathies and enlarged his outlook. What he lost in fiery zeal he gained in geniality. He had a constant perception of the truth that outward things are an index to inner conditions and correspond with them. This prompted him to observe the faces of his fellow-creatures and to attempt a system of physiognomy. His instinctive reading of faces was often astonishingly correct ; but his makeshift system has no value. More to the point are his aphorisms, which were read and annotated by Blake, and these are sufficient both to reveal Lavater and bring certain lasting convictions of Blake's into a clear light. I will take a few of the more important.

Sin and destruction of order are the same.

Blake comments : " A golden sentence." He had felt for many years that all repression was futile. What is repressed comes out again in the wrong place. The last state of the repressed man is worse than his first. Blake was not yet quite clear about what was the alternative to repression, but he was sure that sin was disorder. How he resolved the disorder we shall see later on.

As the interest of man, so his God. As his God, so he.

Blake: " All gold."

He preferred the word " will " to " interest." " Will " is identical with Swedenborg's " affection " and Boehme's

" desire." No one has worked out the correspondence of the " heart " with the " will " so effectually as Swedenborg. Blake knew that to discover the will was to discover the man. A man can change only as he changes the object of his will. When his will is towards God, his powers fall into order and he becomes a saint.

The greatest of characters no doubt would be he who, free of all trifling accidental helps, could see objects through one grand immutable medium always at hand and proof against illusion and time, reflecting every object in its true shape and colour, through all the fluctuation of things.

Blake : " This was Christ."

He knew both as an artist and a mystic that the appearance of objects is according to the state of the beholder. This is true of the objects not only of the outer world but also of the inner, and therefore only the witness of a perfect man is trustworthy. The visions of all others must be corrected by the vision of the Christ.

Who has witnessed one free and unrestrained act of yours has witnessed all.

Underlined by Blake.

Strained action was an abhorrence to Blake. Only those acts are beautiful that are impulsive, and they are they that reveal the man.

Between the best and the worst there are, you say, innumerable degrees—and you are right. But admit that I am right too in saying that the best and the worst differ only in one thing—in the object of their love.

Blake : " Would to God that every one would consider this."

It was considered and maintained by Swedenborg, Boehme, Fénelon, and constantly by St Catherine of Siena, who to the " God is Love " of St John added " Man is love also."

Keep him at least three paces distant who hates bread, music, and the laugh of a child.

Blake : " The best in the book."

He who adores an impersonal God has none, and without guide or rudder launches on an immense abyss that first absorbs his powers and next himself.

Blake : " Most superlatively beautiful, and most affectionately holy and pure.   Would to God that all men would consider it."

His faith in a personal God was his lifelong inspiration in religion and art.   This must guard him against the charge of pantheism made against him by the Swedenborgian Garth Wilkinson and our fleshly poet Swinburne.   Yet he never thought out his position clear of pantheism.   Swedenborg worshipped a personal God and regarded man and nature as emanations from God removed by varying degrees.   But no matter how many degrees, continuous or discrete, one removes ultimates from God, yet if they are essentially emanations from Him, they must be of the same substance, and this is pantheism.   Catholic theology has grappled far more effectually with this ancient difficulty than either Swedenborg or Blake.

All abstraction is temporary folly.

Blake : " I once thought otherwise, but now I know it is truth." Let those who confound mysticism with abstraction note this.

Blake perceived in Lavater the innocence of a child, and loved him accordingly ; but he had already surpassed him, and thus was able to criticize him with true discernment. He said that Lavater made " everything originate in its accident." But a man's sins are accidents and not a part of his real nature. They are a denial of his real man, and therefore are negative. Hence he says : " Vice is a great negation. Every man's leading propensity ought to be called his leading Virtue and his good Angel." This last sentence contains Nietzsche. Every positive act is virtue. Murder, theft, backbiting, undermining, circumventing, are vicious because they are not positive acts, but prevent them in the perpetrator and the victim. He put his finger on Lavater's other mistake, which was also shared by his contemporaries. " They suppose that Woman's Love is Sin. In consequence, all the loves and graces, with them, are sins." Blake not only here outstrips his contemporaries, but at a leap reaches what are the conclusions of the twentieth century. In the nineteenth, men and women racked their brains over the irreconcilable dualism of art and religion, and they chose one or the other, with baneful results. Blake reconciled the two when he saw that the new man in us, unveiled by regeneration, worked by direct vision (religion), and that the new man's prime quality was imagination (art). Once he grasped this, the problem ceased for him.

Here we get at the reason why Lavater has ever failed to keep his lovers. Moses Mendelssohn, disciplined in the severe scholastic methods of Maimonides, easily vanquished him in religious controversy ; but men who were less directly concerned with his religion, like Goethe, began by exaggerating his qualities and ended by quietly dropping him. It is clear to us that Lavater could keep our allegiance only if he had taken a big step forward in the same direction as Blake. This was impossible, and so we find ourselves obliged to follow Goethe's example.

Swedenborg's influence was the greatest and most lasting on Blake's mind.

It is not clear when Blake first took to reading Swedenborg. There is no trace of his influence until *The Songs of Innocence and Experience*. Some of Swedenborg's early scientific works had been translated into English. But of his theological works only one volume out of twelve of the *Arcana Celestia* was published in English ; and, for the rest, those who could not read Latin had to be content with samples. Since Swedenborg bulked so largely in Blake's life, it is necessary to give here some details of his mental and spiritual development.

Swedenborg's father was a Lutheran Bishop. Thus the son, in his most impressionable years, was thrown among Lutherans, who maintained a strenuous protest against the errors of the papacy, and fed or starved their souls with dreary doctrines of justification by faith only, imputed righteousness, and other forensic privileges that came to them through the substitutionary death and merits of Christ. In all these dogmas the young Swedenborg was well drilled. But his first bent was in quite another direction. While still a boy he manifested a scientific mind of immense energy and curiosity that peered searchingly into all the sciences of his time, and won for himself a wonderful knowledge of anatomy, astronomy, mathematics, mechanics, chemistry, mineralogy, and led him to make interesting experiments in invention, such as water-clocks and flying machines. He wrote many books on these subjects, the best known of which in England is *The Animal Kingdom*. Here his interest is greatly stirred by things physical and psychological, and he is fired with the ambition to unite the two. Not, however, till he was fifty-four did his first interest pass over to the things of the soul. When this transition took place, he peered with the same intense scrutiny into supersensual things, and brought to bear on them a mind formed and informed by science and scientific methods.

He took up the Lutheran tenets precisely where he had left them, but, no longer a child, he was forced to criticize what he had once felt, and he set himself to rationalize Lutheran theology and such elements of catholic theology as had survived through Luther. In this he was not always so successful as he imagined. His doctrine of the Trinity, that Jesus Christ is the One God and that the Trinity is in Him, gets over an arithmetical difficulty, but finally leaves the imagination baffled, trying to make out how Jesus carried on the government of the universe while He lay a helpless infant in the manger or His mother's arms. His reaction against all outside views of Christ's death, imputed righteousness, and faith only, was more successful, but not new, since in this the quakers in England and Jacob Boehme were before him. Nor was his contention that love was the supreme good new to those who had read through the New Testament. His doctrine of uses was merely a theological variation of that utilitarianism which is inseparable from rationalism, and which casts over everything a drab veil that only the artist can remove. He is really at his best when he expatiates on love and wisdom. Love correponds with the heart, wisdom with the lungs. As the heart sends the blood to the lungs, where it is purified by the oxygen, so love feeds the understanding, and is in turn purified by it. Swedenborg's perception of wisdom begotten of love inspired his best passages and gave them their authentic import.

Swedenborg gazed inwards so intently that after an initial period of unrest, terrors, and nightmares his inner eye opened, and he saw into the realities of the inner world. For the moment

I take his word for it, and will question later on.   His open eye saw into heaven and hell, gazed into the faces of angels and of God, and his opened ear heard the angels speaking things he could understand and utter.   At once he rationalized.   He stripped even the celestial angels of all mystery as well as of garments, and traced them back to an earthly pedigree.   Angels are men, and when they talk they are no more interesting than the elders of a Lutheran congregation.   God also is a man—not, be it observed, the Man of a crude anthropomorphism, but infinite, omnipotent Man, from Whom each man, created in His image (will) and likeness (understanding), draws his real manhood.   He carried this doctrine into his rationalized version of the Incarnation.   Christ assumed human nature in the womb of the Virgin, and by His conquering life put it off, replacing it by the Divine Humanity.   The last phrase has accomplished yeasty work in modern religious thought. How many are aware of its origin ?

Swedenborg throws out many suggestive remarks about hell.   Certainly it was high time that it was looked into, for the protestant hell was as horrible and revolting as the catholic.   He began by lifting himself out of space and time.   He was soon brought by necessity to perceive that when these no longer exist, then all appearances depend upon a man's state, and therefore state governs the perceptions whether of the angels in heaven or the devils in hell.   Hell, like heaven, is peopled entirely from earth.   No one goes there but by his own choice, and he chooses because he finds there exactly what is congenial to his own condition.   Swedenborg eliminated anything arbitrary in man's destiny. Fitness decides by an inexorable law that God could evade only by ceasing to be God.   Swedenborg's hell is a filthy and insanitary place, but the filthy inhabitants are no more disturbed by that than rats in a sewer. He further declared that heaven and hell were born together, and that they are contraries necessary to each other's existence. Blake underlined and commented on this in his copy of the *Angelic Wisdom concerning the Divine Love*. How the suggestion worked in him we shall see later on.

Swedenborg's hell is filthy and his heaven dull. There are further surprises when we through his mediumship glimpse their inhabitants. The angels, of course, are all sound Swedenborgians, and are attractive or repellent according to Swedenborg's attraction or repulsion for us. But the devils, not being Swedenborgians, can command an audience of the majority of Christians who agree with them in their non-allegiance. What Blake discovered in them was a wonderful energy and exuberance which made them not only more attractive than the angels, but also, except for the stenches, might almost have transformed their hell into heaven.

By this time Swedenborg had explored many kingdoms— mineral, vegetable, animal, human, divine, hellish; and his knowledge of the kingdoms informed him of universal correspondences, the law of which came to him thus freshly from his own observation. It was probably this which made him assert so often that he was announcing something new, for with his culture he must have known that Paracelsus had perceived the same law like hundreds before him, and that Boehme wrote a treatise on the *Signatures* of all things.

Perhaps Swedenborg's most fruitful apprehension was that of the Divine Influx. All creatures live as they receive out of the Divine fullness. They have no inherent or self-existent life of their own. The Lord alone is self-existent, and they live by a derived life. This happens to be catholic theology too, and it kept Swedenborg away from a misty pantheism. Men and angels live, move, and have their being in God. They are immersed in an ocean of life and light which pours forth from the Lord of the Universe. The moment they feel their need and are humble enough to turn to the Lord they become receptive. Filled with the spirit of life and light, they love and understand, and remain full so long as they humbly abide in Him. Perhaps no modern has grasped this truth so completely as Swedenborg. It almost made him a mystic. Almost, yet not quite, for his fundamental desire was to bring all the mysteries of the faith down to the level of man's understanding. He eschewed a faith that rested on what could not be understood. He did not see that in tearing away veil after veil he turned heaven along with earth into a laboratory. The true mystic loves to know that all things, including his faith, run up into mystery; and if an angel succeeded in laying bare the last mystery, the mystic would find himself in hell.

Swedenborg attempted to bring reason and order into things spiritual, and he believed that he had succeeded ; but what really happened was that he confounded the workings of his own subliminal mind with the action of the Lord's, and in 1775, when he had effected reason and order in the intermediate world of spirits to his own satisfaction, he declared that the last judgment had taken place, that the New Jerusalem had descended down out of Heaven, and that he was the divinely appointed prophet of the New Church.

He was not long publishing the doctrine of the New Church concerning the Sacred Scriptures. He knew as well as any modern critic what are the difficulties in the way of accepting the doctrine of verbal inspiration, yet he affirmed it. There is a further difficulty that we feel more acutely than he in the protestant dogma

" the Bible and the Bible only."   If we are cut off from memory or tradition, and are obliged to form our image of the historical Jesus from the Bible only, it is next to impossible to make that image shine forth with clear, sharp outlines.   The difficulty is still further increased when protestantism, pushed to its logical extreme, eliminates the supernatural element, and tries to piece together the character of Jesus from the fragments that remain.

The Bible imperiously demands a theory that shall make its heterogeneous contents cohere.   The four evangelists presuppose a knowledge of Jesus that they aim at making more perfect.   These are difficulties that protestantism was destined to feel acutely from the day it proudly rejected tradition.   No doubt, if Providence had so intended, the portrait of Jesus would have been drawn so completely that without the aid of memory we could have gained a knowledge of Him such as we have of no other man that ever lived.   But the fact remains that Jesus wrote no book and no letters, and He founded nothing but a handful of illiterate disciples to preach His gospel and perpetuate His memory. These were so confident that Israel would repent and believe the Gospel, and so make possible the immediate return of their Lord, that they never thought of taking to their pens ; and it was only when they grew alarmed at the increasing thinness of the apostolic ranks that they committed their memories to wise scribes or to parchment.   Thus we owe the Gospel accounts not to the express commands of Jesus, but to the first bitter disappointment of the apostolic band.

The simple truth, of course, is that the New Testament Scriptures cannot be understood apart from the Catholic Faith that gave them birth, and therefore when the faith is not confessed a theory must be found to take its place.

The history of higher criticism is the history of a succession of theories. Dr Paulus, forgotten father of German critics, supplied a rational one, for which he was obliged to make a super-historical use of the Essenes. It has reappeared in George Moore's *Brook Kerith*.

Renan, pantheist, artist and sceptic, tried to supply a subjective artistic explanation which soothed the subject, but turned the Object into a Frenchman. Strauss, Keim and Bousset, learned and painstaking, with hardly less success made Him into a dreamy cosmopolitan German of a now obsolete type. Schweitzer, better informed of the apocalyptic and eschatological medium through which the mind of Jesus worked, comes nearer to the apostolic mind that drew the picture of Jesus, yet, for want of the key, portrays Jesus as the tragic victim of the illusory time-spirit.

Swedenborg never gave any serious consideration to the catholic theory, but supplied its place out of the store of his supersensual revelations. Loaded with these, and with a vague memory of the gnostic teaching of the threefold meaning of the Scriptures, he was able to evade every literal difficulty by turning to the spiritual meaning, and if need be to the celestial, which could be reached only through his own specific revelation. It is true that he tried to bring a steadying factor into his subjective interpretation by introducing his doctrine of correspondences ; but as he has never been able to convince any but his elect followers that his correspondences, beyond some obvious ones, are other than arbitrary, he has succeeded only in making his commentaries on Genesis, Exodus, and the Apocalypse unreadable to the vast majority of Christians.

I have said enough about Swedenborg to make it clear that there was some affinity between him and Blake.

Blake's imperfect knowledge of him was much deepened in 1788, when he read his *Angelic Wisdom concerning the Divine Love and concerning the Divine Wisdom*. This he marked and annotated, and so we are able to trace the affinity in considerable detail.

On the whole Blake gives almost passionate approval to *The Angelic Wisdom*. Only in rare instances does he differ. Swedenborg's doctrine of state made explicit what Blake had vaguely perceived all his life. It also helped him to formulate a theoretic explanation of his own supersensual vision. This is so important that I must quote an entire paragraph from *The Angelic Wisdom*, for the sake of Blake's comment and the reader's understanding.

69. THE DIVINE FILLS ALL THE SPACES OF THE UNIVERSE APART FROM SPACE. *There are two things proper to nature, SPACE and TIME. Out of these man in the natural world forms the ideas of his thought and therefore his understanding. If he remains in these ideas and does not raise his mind above them he is nowise able to perceive anything spiritual and Divine, for he involves them in ideas which derive from space and time ; and in proportion as he does this, the light—the lumen—of his understanding becomes merely natural. To think from the lumen in reasoning about spiritual and Divine things, is like thinking from the thick darkness of night concerning the things which appear only in the light of day. This is the origin of naturalism. But he who knows how to raise his mind above the ideas of thought which derive from space and time, passes from thick darkness into light, and apprehends spiritual and Divine things, and, at last, sees those things which are in them and from them, and then by virtue of that light he disperses the thick darkness of the natural lumen, and*

relegates its fallacies from the middle to the sides.   Every man with an understanding is able to think, and actually does think, above those properties of nature; and then he affirms and sees that the Divine, being omnipresent, is not in space.   He is also able to affirm and to see those things which have been adduced above.   But if he denies the Divine Omnipresence and ascribes all things to nature, then he is not willing to be elevated, although he is able.

In the above Blake changed the word *middle* into *centre*, and *sides* into *circumference*, commenting : " When the fallacies of darkness are in the circumference they cast a bound about the infinite."   In paragraph 70, Swedenborg adds what is a corollary to the above : *Angels do not comprehend when we say that the divine fills spaces, for they do not know what spaces are, but they understand when we say that the divine fills all things.*   On this Blake makes the comment " Excellent."

Since the inhabitants of heaven have no idea of space and time, their perceptions and modes of thought are entirely governed by their state.   This is true also of the visionary, and it decides what he reports of the other world.   Everyone will easily perceive from this of what paramount importance his state is in assigning the right value to his visions.   As Swedenborg says : " Spaces and times in spiritual life have relation to states of love and are mutable with these."

Blake fully approved of Swedenborg's doctrine that the heart and lungs correspond to the will and understanding.   Those who would understand Blake must remember this while reading the prophetic books.

But there are signs of disagreements that deepened with time.

Swedenborg wrote (237) : *Man at birth comes first into the natural degree, and this increases in him by continuity, according to his various knowledge . . . until he reaches the highest point of the understanding which is called the rational. But still the second degree, which is the spiritual, is not opened by this means. This is opened by love towards the neighbour . . . the third degree by love towards the Lord.*

With all Blake's devout admiration for Swedenborg this was too much for him. A child born solely into the natural degree ! That ! after all Blake knew, and all Christ had said about little children ! Heaven save us all, especially Swedenborg ! Blake's comment is important. Note that even when he is differing from his teacher, his language is Swedenborgian. He says :

" Study science till you are blind. Study intellectuals until you are cold. Yet science cannot teach intellect. Much less can intellect teach affection. How foolish it is then to assert that man is born in only one degree, when that one degree is receptive of the three degrees : two of which he must destroy or close up or they will descend. If he closes up the two superior, then he is not truly in the third but descends out of it into mere Nature or Hell. Is it not also evident that one degree will not open the other, and that science will not open intellect, but that they are discrete and not continuous so as to explain each other, except by correspondence, which has nothing to do with demonstration, for you cannot demonstrate one degree by the other, for how can science be brought to demonstrate intellect without making them continuous and not discrete ? "

There are three comments in which Blake introduces an element lacking in the voluminous writings of Swedenborg. On Swedenborg's statement : " A spiritual idea does not derive anything from space, but it derives its all from state," he remarks : " *Poetic* idea " ; on paragraph 10, Blake comments : " He who loves feels love descend into him, and if he is wise, may perceive it from the *Poetic Genius*, which is the Lord " ; on Swedenborg's phrase : " The negation of God constitutes hell," he remarks : " The negation of the *Poetic Genius*."

Here we get a hint of a small seed of difference which when fully grown was to sever Blake from Swedenborg for ever.

I must give one more, very pregnant, passage from *The Angelic Wisdom*.

68. Man out of his hereditary evil reacts against God. But if he believes that all his life is from God, and all good of life from the action of God, and all evil of life from the reaction of man, then reaction becomes the offspring of action, and man acts with God as from himself. The equilibrium of all things is from action and joint reaction, and everything must be in equilibrium.

The last sentence makes hell an eternal necessity to preserve the equilibrium of heaven. Strictly it makes also the devil an eternal counterweight to God, and what else follows we may learn by studying Zoroastrian dualism. Blake's comment was : " God and evil are here both good, and the two contraries married."

Blake was early occupied with the marriage of contraries. Swedenborg's word was a sanguine seed in prepared soil, and when it brought forth fruit a hundredfold, the rich return was not the logical outcome of Swedenborg's dualism, but a marriage of heaven and hell, of religion and art, which is showing a fertile capacity for endless reproduction.

E

So far, then, Swedenborg's attraction for Blake far exceeded his repulsion, and he embraced him with impetuous affection. Here was a teacher who could understand by experience both the new birth and vision. By his help he disentangled himself from the particular explanation and theory of the atonement as given by Whitefield and Wesley. Here was a visionary who could not only understand his own visions, but who could give a reasonable explanation of the working of the visionary faculty. Swedenborg brought order, reason, and system into Blake's chaotic mind. Isolated from the churches, yet ardently desiring fellowship as the substance of his faith and wisdom, it appeared to him that there was nothing else to do but join the New Church of Swedenborg, and accordingly, in 1788, he and Catherine signed their names in token of membership and assent to the distinctive doctrines of the New Church. The curious may find this reported in the Minutes of the first Seven Sessions of the General Conference of the New Church, published by James Speirs, 36 Bloomsbury Street, 1885.

Let us turn to Blake's two poems, *Tiriel*, 1788, and *Thel*, 1789, which have special interest as they were written about this time that he subscribed to the Swedenborgian Church and Swedenborg's influence was paramount.

Tiriel—old, bald, and blind—is related to Urizen, but Urizen in Blake's completed mythology is the symbol not only of the law with its prohibitive commandments, but of the reason formed by the five senses, and therefore ever ready to stamp out imagination and inspiration, which derive their source from beyond the senses. Tiriel is the product of the law, and is the antithesis of love. Swedenborg's natural man was justified and saved by love, Luther's faith not being sufficient, and so in Blake's Tiriel there is besides St Paul's law the Lutheran's pharisaism, and just a suggestion of that contempt for the beautiful which was to make Urizen such a terrible figure, and was eventually to lead to Blake's estrangement from Swedenborg.

Tiriel at the hour of his death realized why his paradise was fallen, and he had found nought but the drear sandy plain. His description of his own upbringing, shocking as it is, is that of the great bulk of mankind. The instant a child is born, the dull, blind father stands ready to form the infant head; and if the child, like Blake, has vision, the father, like Mr Blake, uses the whip to rouse the sluggish senses to act and to scourge off all youthful fancies.

"Then walks the weak infant in sorrow, compelled to number footsteps
  Upon the sand. And when the drone has reached his crawling length,
  Black berries appear that poison all round him. Such was Tiriel
  Compelled to pray repugnant, and to humble the immortal spirit ;
  Till I am subtle as a serpent in a paradise,
  Consuming all, both flowers and fruits, insects and warbling birds."

Blake was thinking of his father and his own early whippings. But really fathers are not absolutely necessary, for the mother, the nurse, the elder sister, and the public school, can do the job a great deal more effectually. The other poem, *The Book of Thel*, 1789, is Swedenborgian throughout. Thel, youngest daughter of the Seraphim, bewails the transitoriness of life and all beautiful things, herself included. Then the *humble* Lily of the Valley, a little Cloud, a Worm, and a Clod of Clay, all in their respective ways preach to her that " Everything that lives, lives not alone nor for itself." When she has reached the utter selflessness of a Clod of Clay, then only will she be able to behold steadfastly the seeming transitoriness of youth and beautiful things ; seeming, for like the lowly lily they melt to flourish in eternal vales.

Here Blake endorses the Swedenborgian selflessness, and extols the Swedenborgian lowliness, modesty, and humility. Swedenborg believed in no doctrine of self-realization. To him the self was always an evil till lost in the Lord. It was the remains in him of German mysticism. Blake slowly and surely came to set a high value on the true self. But unlike the more modern preacher of self-realization, he believed that a man found his real self only after he had given himself passionately to Jesus the eternal life and the eternal imagination. Then he was no longer to value the humility and modesty attached to selflessness. Their place was to be taken by a new kind of humility and a new kind of modesty of such flaming quality, that he wished to drop the old names and find others that more nearly described their sovereign reality.

Thel is finally invited by the matron Clay to enter her house, with the assurance that she may return. Immediately the terrific Porter of the Eternal Gates lifted the *northern* bar.

This is a well-known gate, among Swedenborgians, into the unseen world. But it is very terrible. According to Garth Wilkinson it was the only gate that Blake knew, and he accounts by this means for Blake's apotheosis of the self and the passions. At this time Blake saw through this gate what Swedenborg saw ; but later, when he had shaken him off and changed his state, his vision changed accordingly, and the objects were stripped of their horror. He was also to know all the four gates leading into the unseen.

Thel, entering, " wandered in the land of clouds through valleys dark, list'ning dolours and lamentations " till she came even to her own grave-plot. Through such a gate it matters not whether one views this world or the other. Both must appear sad and joyless in the extreme, and enmesh the beholder in blackest pessimism. Thel, hearing a voice wailing like the ecclesiastic dirge of the disillusioned King, shrieked with terror, and fled back unhindered into the vales of Har.

Thel is sweet, even heavenly in the Swedenborgian sense. But its sweetness cloys. Christ, like the Law before Him, made a sparing use of honey, preferring the more indispensable salt, which He enjoined His disciples to have in themselves at all times. Blake was to recover plentiful salt, but not until he had drawn Swedenborg's line between heaven and hell in a wholly different place.

Swedenborg's influence is pleasantly found at work in the *Songs of Innocence*. Innocence was a favourite word, and Swedenborg saw the celestial angels both innocent and naked. There is nothing more innocent than a lamb, and therefore Blake by a sure instinct and in childlike joy piped his song about the lamb, satisfying at once his feeling for the lamb, the child, and the Maker of the lamb who was called the Lamb of God.

The song called *The Divine Image* shows Swedenborg's influence at its best. So many men with Blake's mystic proclivities rush into vague abstractions. To-day we hear of Infinite Love and Infinite Wisdom, Infinite Life, and all personality denied to God. Yet these are mere high-sounding abstractions, and are quite meaningless apart from concrete personality. Swedenborg was clear as day here, and it was he who taught Blake the pure wisdom contained in his verses :

" For Mercy, Pity, Peace, and Love
Is God, our Father dear,
And Mercy, Pity, Peace, and Love
Is man, His child and care.

For Mercy has a human heart,
Pity a human face,
And Love, the human form divine,
And Peace, the human dress."

Swedenborg's teaching continues in *The Songs of Experience*, but with a question mark.

Blake sings to the Fly :

" Am not I
A fly like thee ?
Or art not thou
A man like me ? "

To see humanity in a fly is Swedenborgian ; and Blake answered his question in the affirmative.

In the next song there are many questions ; and it cannot be doubted that Blake's answers would have been the exact contrary to Swedenborg's.

Swedenborg, like his theosophical predecessors, had a way of denying that God created the particular animals that man finds inconvenient. Tigers, wolves, rats, bats, and moths are so obnoxious, that it soothes man's vanity to suppose that they are embodiments of evil exhaled from hell. They have served as restful homes for vampires and other creations of Old Night. And so Swedenborg, governed by mental habits of reason and use as measured by man, drew a sharp line between animals of a heavenly and hellish origin. When Blake saw the tiger he saw differently.

His æsthetic eye instantly marvelled at its " fearful symmetry," the fire of its eyes, the sinews of its heart ; and he cried, " Did He who made the Lamb make thee?" He gives no answer. But there was no need. " In what distant *deeps* or *skies*" the tiger had his origin had no further perplexity for him once he had married hell to heaven.

The Little Vagabond, though hardly within the ken of Swedenborg, contains what every vagabond knows. Blake was able to rescue vagabonds as well as tigers from an exclusively hellish origin.

Blake remained an orthodox Swedenborgian for nearly two years, and then came reaction and rebellion, not without resentment and bitterness. What was the cause of Blake's permanent repudiation of Swedenborg? Various reasons are given by Swedenborgians to prove that Blake was wholly in the wrong. Mr Morris gives a beautifully simple explanation. Quoting Blake's saying that he had two different states, one in which he liked Swedenborg's writings and one in which he disliked them, he says, " The latter was a state of pride in himself, and then they were distasteful to him, but afterwards he knew that he had not been wise and sane." That is the way that we all at some time in our life account for the obstinacy of those who will not worship at our altar.

Mr Garth Wilkinson, who of Swedenborgians most deserves to be heard, wrote in the preface of his edition of *The Songs of Innocence and Experience*, 1839, that Blake entered the " invisible world through the terrific porter of its northern gate." Like Shelley, he verged towards pantheism, not a spiritual pantheism, but a " natural spiritualism " or " ego-theism." His genius " entered into and inhabited the Egyptian and Asiatic perversions of an ancient and true religion," and thus " found a home in the ruins of Ancient and consummated Churches." Wilkinson discovered a great deal of the ego and of hell in Blake. All of this criticism, which is ingenious, I cannot accept. To begin with the ego. Swedenborg believed that every man in his own *proprium* was consumed with self-love, and that only love to the Lord could enable him entirely to overcome his love of self. Blake believed that the real self was made in the image of God, and therefore it must be loved, reverenced, and obeyed. The recognition of the same divine principle in others enables one to love one's neighbour as oneself. All German mystical talk of hatred to self and death to self was repudiated by Blake as artificial and unreal.

It is true that Blake came nearer to pantheism than Swedenborg did. He had come, through his teacher, to regard the universe as an emanation from God, and in working from this doctrine to its logical outcome in pantheism he was more consistent than Swedenborg, who tried to evade the consequences of his own theory.

That Blake found a home in an ancient and consummated Church is true only if Swedenborg's New Church is really the New Jerusalem predicted by St John ! For the rest, we hail with joy the element of " hell " in Blake.

Blake himself makes some short incisive remarks on Swedenborg, which will carry us a little farther to an understanding. " Swedenborg has not written one new truth." " He has written all the old falsehoods." Blake had ardently welcomed Swedenborg as a new teacher with a new message. In these sentences he betrays disappointment, anger, and resentment. " Any man of mechanical talents may, from the writings of Paracelsus or Jacob Behmen, produce ten thousand volumes of equal value with Swedenborg's, and from those of Dante or Shakespeare an infinite number." If Blake had had a wider culture, he would have known this when a boy, and blown off his fumes at the proper season. We shall encounter again and again his lack of grace when dealing with his successful contemporaries.

We see, so far, that Blake reckoned that Swedenborg had failed him, and that anything of value he found in him, he could find in the old masters. But there was something he could find in them—a spirit of beauty and a beauty of form—that was wholly lacking in Swedenborg, and an energy and exuberance that appeared only in Swedenborg's hell. That this should be the net result of Blake's expectations and Swedenborg's pretensions was too much for Blake's patience; hence the violence of his reaction.

Blake must have felt vaguely all along the lack of the æsthetic faculty in Swedenborg. It was Swedenborg who helped him finally to understand the exact value of his visions and thus to place him.

We have seen that Swedenborg, by abstraction from space and time, arrived at a doctrine of state which takes their place in heaven and hell. From this it follows that man's vision is wholly dependent on his state, and also that a man's visions cannot be trusted unless he has a perfect organ of vision resting on a sound state. It is always fatuous for a religious teacher to appeal to his visions to enforce his doctrines, since they depend on the man himself, and we must form our judgment of him apart from his visions. To appeal to a vision for the truth of a doctrine, and to the doctrine for the truth of a vision, is merely to whirl oneself round in a vicious circle; and therefore Swedenborg's whole make-up—will and understanding—must be laid bare and measured by some standard with which we may try the spirits and the prophets before we can begin to approach his visions and gauge their value.

Swedenborg's state was a state of reason, whether he viewed this world or the other. His early scientific studies, unbalanced by any real appreciation of art, moulded his mind into a rigid state which was impervious to any outside stimulus. When he turned to religion, he made the barren attempt to trim the mysteries of the Faith until they came wholly within the grasp of the understanding. This is a rationalizing process. Swedenborgians may object to hear their master called a rationalist. It is true that that term is usually applied to those who have no supersensual vision, and even deny its existence. Swedenborg is, of course, sharply distinguished from all such, but he has with them the same fundamental trust of reason, which in their case is used to gauge the things of this world, in his the things of the other. Hence when he has raised our expectations to a dizzy height, as he is about to report on things seen and heard in heaven and hell, there is a ludicrous anticlimax when we find that the angels are simply religious and talk theology everlastingly, that heaven is like a well arranged Dutch tulip field, and excepting one or two phases of hell the whole is just as exciting as a problem in Euclid and as dull as a sanitary report. Hell alone stirred some interest because its inmates had energy and blood. And therefore one sympathizes with those spirits who, allowed to peep into heaven, immediately chose to plunge themselves head-first into hell.

Now Blake, being a visionary, knew that vision depended on will, and he learnt further from Swedenborg that it depended also on state, and so, as a man's state changed, his vision changed also. Blake's state was the imagination of the poetic genius (Los), Swedenborg's the dry logical faculty of the unassisted reason (Urizen), and as Blake looked at Swedenborg's heaven and hell, he saw them approaching one to the other and finally with an impetuous rush locked in a marital embrace.

This is the most significant vision of modern times, after which it is easy to judge Swedenborg. He had given for life, theology ; for beauty, ashes ; and instead of emancipating the modern world he condemned it to the appalling tedium of an everlasting Sunday School. The doctrine of the New Jerusalem was not half so beautiful as that of the Old Jerusalem. Christ come again in Glory was stripped of that beauty that men had perceived in His first lowly coming. Blake's indictment of Swedenborg was severe. It was also an indictment of the whole of protestant theology. The magnificent fruit of Swedenborg's action and reaction, attraction and repulsion for Blake was *The Marriage of Heaven and Hell.* Blake was fresh from reading Swedenborg's *Heaven and Hell,* and this and not the ecclesiastical was continually in his thought as he wrote. At the same time it is necessary to remember that Blake was not merely criticizing Swedenborg. Swedenborg gave a rationalized version of the Lutheran doctrine, and therefore to reject him involved a rejection of much of Luther's teaching and of the protestantism that has flowed from him.

Heaven, then, consists of the passive obeyers of reason, the religious, the good ; hell of the active obeyers of Energy, the irreligious, the evil. Here let it be well marked and remembered that by the religious Blake always meant those who repress their energies or passions until they become passive enough for them to obey reason.

Hell's prime quality is passion or energy or desire. This in itself is neither good nor evil in the abstract sense in which these words are generally understood, but considered absolutely it is good, for it is the native energy of the man made in God's image and likeness. Energy works according to the object of desire. If a man's object is the flesh, he becomes an adulterer ; if things of beauty and delight, an artist ; if God, a saint. Religious people, frightened and mistrustful of their desires, restrain them until they are passive, and in doing so they are destroying the motive power of their lives. They are wholly successful when they become dead souls, and it is then, strictly speaking, that they are fit, not for heaven, but for hell. The stronger the desire, the greater the man. Once direct the energy by fixing its desire on God, it will drive the man to greatness. Thus the typical restrainer or devil is the priest, the typical man of passion or energy is the artist. Those who restrain their energies in the name of Christ have identified Him with the reason, and they have never caught so much as a glimpse of Him as He is. Swedenborg and Milton worshipped a rational Christ, and therefore in Blake's eyes, as also in the catholic's, they were heretics. The Book of Job and Shakespeare see inspiration and imagination working with energy as the highest good. The restrainer in the Book of Job is called Satan. Blake alone in his time saw Christ as the supreme symbol of the passionate-imaginative life.

Those who have followed Blake thus far will at once understand the Proverbs of Hell, and perceive in them the glorification of energy and all things belonging to it. Excess, pride, lust and wrath are evidences of great energy. Therefore " the road of *excess* leads to the palace of wisdom," " the *pride* of the peacock is the glory of God," " the *lust* of the goat is the bounty of God " "the *wrath* of the lion is the wisdom of God." Generosity, prodigality, open-handedness, impulse, show a rich full nature. Prudence, number, measure, weight, betray poverty and are fit "in a year of death." The animals of abounding energy are the noblest, like the lion, tiger, eagle. The animals lacking great energy take refuge in cunning, like the fox and the crow. (Blake no longer questions who made the tiger.) Blake extols fountains, not cisterns or standing water, courage not cunning, exuberance not reason-broken passion. Even an energetic "damn" braces, while a pious blessing induces a flabby relaxation.

Man's most valuable gift of God is passion. What a man makes of his life will depend on how he regards his passion, and into what channels he directs its course.

Thus Blake unites contraries. But just as all is going merry as a marriage bell, he suddenly declares that there are some contraries that can never be married. The modern immanentist world is trying to unite good and evil, beauty and ugliness, with baneful results. We are told that there is nothing ugly to the discerning eye, and one wonders why one should take pains to improve ones crude daubs. Blake says that religious people are always trying to make these false matches. He gives as a typical example the prolific and devourer—the active and passive. Each is necessary to the other's existence. Union destroys both. It is easy to multiply examples. Black and white produce grey, beautiful in art, but depressing in life. Dark and light, twilight, beautiful, but sad and lowering. Cold and heat, lukewarmness, which is hateful. Hard and soft, slush, which abounds in modern thought. Hate and love, unctuousness or slime, which is particularly obnoxious in some religious people.

Blake hated these mashes. He had no faith in the love that could not hate. Just as he seemed on the brink of sweeping away hell like an amiable modern, he discovered that though he had made quick work of the Swedenborgian and protestant hell, yet hell as Christ thought of it remained and must remain. "Note.—Jesus Christ did not wish to unite, but to separate them, as in the Parable of sheep and goats. And He says, ' I come not to send Peace, but a Sword.'" Thus Blake kept his perception clear and sharp. In following his own mental energy he was able to shake off all pantheistic distortions of good and evil, and to see that though with the majority these are mere abstractions, yet there is ultimately an eternal distinction between them, and therefore heaven and earth may pass away, but Jesus Christ's word concerning heaven and hell will abide for ever.

Christians have thought of heaven and hell too much as of future places. Blake thought of them primarily as present states. Here a man's state is obscured by its intermingling with conditions of space and time. Hereafter the state creates the environment. The man in a state of hell, and therefore in hell, is the one whose energy or vital fire is dead. The man in a state of Heaven is the one who lives the more abundant life in which his religion, art, and philosophy have become one. The real hell and the real heaven can never be married, for any attempt to marry them results in moral loss. But a man can pass from a state of hell into a state of heaven, and the way to do it is the old way of repentance and faith—repentance which changes heart and mind by giving them a new object, and faith that takes and receives the glad tidings of the Kingdom of God.

Blake gave a curious illustration of his doctrine of state. A Swedenborgian angel came to him, and condoled with him because of the hot, burning dungeon that he was preparing for himself to all eternity. The angel at his request undertook to show him his place in hell. Truly it was horrible, and Blake describes the ideal Swedenborgian hell with a power and vividness to which Swedenborg could never attain. The angel, not enjoying the sight, decamped ; but no sooner was Blake alone than the horrible vision vanished, and he found himself " on a pleasant bank beside a river, by moonlight, hearing a harper, who sung to the harp." The angel had drawn him into his state, and he saw what the angel saw. When he regained his real state, the vision was pleasant enough. Afterwards he rejoined the angel and undertook to show him his lot. An angel is necessarily above the modes of space and time. This one being religious, and therefore repressed to passivity, was shown a timeless, spaceless void, which was an eternal nightmare more unutterably fearful than anything in Swedenborg's filthy sewer.

Finally Blake overheard a marvellously rich and splendid bit of conversation between a devil in a flame of fire and an angel seated on a cloud.

The devil pointed out how Jesus Christ was obedient to impulse, and how His obedience to His passionate energies—to the Voice of God within Him—made Him the Great Rebel and Law Breaker, mocking the sabbath and the sabbath's God, guilty of the blood of His martyrs, exonerating the woman taken in adultery, living on the labour and sweat of wage-slaves, acquiescing in a false witness by His silence, coveting the best gifts for His disciples. It was a Pharisee who said, " All these laws have I kept from my youth," and he became a dead soul. Jesus on the cross looked back on a pathway strewn with the corpses of the religious people He had killed in His fiery impetuous course, and instead of a death-repentance, He uttered the audacious word, " Father, into Thy Hands I commend My Spirit."

The angel was converted. Embracing the flame of fire he was consumed, and rose again as Elijah—the prophet of spirit and fire.

And thus Blake took his leave of Swedenborg. He had expected too much of him and was disappointed. It was more than enough to hear his name on the lips of his pious, commonplace brother. He was indignant that he had not fulfilled·his high-sounding pretensions, and " the voice of honest indignation," he wrote, " is the voice of God." But we who calmly look on can detect the voice of resentment too, which robs his departure of grace. But for Swedenborg *The Marriage of Heaven and Hell* had never been written. Swedenborg was the Goliath, strong in reason, logic, system, science, intellect, slain by the stone from David's sling. Blake and not Swedenborg was " the true Samson shorn by the Churches."

CHAPTER VI

THE REBELS

BLAKE was thirty-three when in 1790 he wrote *The Marriage of Heaven and Hell*.

It marked a crisis in his life. Hitherto, with all the generous exuberance of youth, he was striving to leave the past behind, and reach forth to something new that by sheer glory and beauty should sweep up in its course the youth of the ages to come.

For a time he believed that Swedenborg could supply him with the fire to fashion and direct his own genius ; but after poring long over his pages, he began reluctantly to discover that the fire of his imagination had either never been kindled or it was long since extinct. Whatever else remained in Swedenborg— and there were undeniably many good things—was impotent for the supreme task of supplying the creative spark.

Blake was disappointed and disillusioned. Never again did he make an impetuous rush to embrace any man, however dazzling his gifts. But not yet had he learnt the vital value of the past. If no new prophet arrived, there was still himself, and if he trusted himself with passionate faith, he might yet accomplish the desired thing.

In 1791 the outer events of his life ran a new course. Some time previously, Fuseli had introduced him to a bookseller and publisher named Johnson, living at 72 St Paul's Churchyard.

This Johnson was a remarkable man. His sympathies were with rebels, whom he detected, welcomed, and encouraged. But he had none of the hard narrowness of advanced liberals, and his eye and heart were quick also to discover and cheer such a shy, diffident, conservative genius as Cowper. He was a friend to the authors whose works he published ; and in a little upper chamber he gave weekly dinner parties, to which were bidden William Godwin, Mary Wollstonecraft, Tom Paine, Dr Price and Dr Priestley, and now Blake himself. In the 'eighties Blake had moved among elegant Blue-stockings who were above all things anxious to show themselves true daughters of Sarah : now in the 'nineties he was one of a party of rebels who despised the past, and were hailing the French Revolution, believing that after a few more of such upheavals a millennium would surely come in which man would be perfected.

Foremost among the rebels was William Godwin. Ten years younger, Blake might have been captivated by Godwin, as later on Shelley, Coleridge, and Bulwer Lytton were to be. There was always something clean and fresh about Godwin, and his hopes and aspirations for mankind were generous. Brought up in the narrowest sect of Calvinism, and believing while still a boy that he was assuredly one of the elect, he rebounded in later life to a liberal humanism, and retained little of his Calvinism except an unshaken belief in his own election. The first edition of his *Enquiry concerning Political Justice* appeared in 1793, in which he stated all his first principles. These can be summarized briefly :

The characters of men originate in their external circumstances, and therefore man has no innate ideas or principles, and no instincts of right action apart from reasoning. Heredity counts for almost nothing. It is impression makes the man. The voluntary actions of men originate in their opinions.

Man is perfectible.

Man has negative rights but no positive rights.

Nothing further is requisite, but the improvement of his reasoning faculty, to make him virtuous and happy. Freedom of will is a curse. It is not free or independent of understanding, and therefore it follows understanding, and fortunately is not free to resist it. Man becomes free as he obeys it. It follows that our disapprobation of vice will be of the same nature as our disapprobation of an infectious distemper.

A scheme of self-love is incompatible with virtue.

The only means by which truth enters is through the inlet of the senses.

Intellect is the creature of sensation, we have no other inlet of knowledge.

Government is in all cases an evil, and it ought to be introduced as sparingly as possible.

Give a state but liberty enough, and it is impossible that vice should exist in it.

Thus Godwin was rationalist, altruist, anarchist, and non-resister. It is not probable that Blake ever read *Political Justice*, his patience not being equal to the task. While ardently desiring political justice and liberty, it was soon plain to him from his personal knowledge of Godwin that all his first principles were false. It was not true that man's character originates in his external circumstances, although these do act on him. The differences between men are traceable to a fundamental inequality. One man turns everything he touches into dross, another into gold. Why? Blake had no need to argue. Being a mystic, he knew that man's innate principles, ideas, and instincts differed, that heredity could not be ignored, that beyond the five inlets of the senses which reason alone recognizes, there are a thousand inlets for the man whose spiritual understanding is awakened.

He shivered at the thought of what the world would become if the rationalist had his way ; for though he would sweep away superstitions, injustices, cruelties, yet from his invariable lack of discrimination he would crush with these the flowers and fruits of imagination, intuition, and inspiration. Besides, whether State or no State, what sort of life would man's be when his fundamental instincts and passions were allowed no expression ? Blake had not the statesman's power of looking at men in the mass, but he knew that the individual was of extreme importance in any community, and also that the individual's value lay in his power of passion, and therefore Godwin's calm, reasoned, *doctrinaire* scheme for bringing the Millennium made no appeal to him whatever, and the two men went their separate courses.

It is interesting to note later that Shelley attained to liberty and song just so far as he shook off Godwin. When he talked with exaggerated nonsense about kings and priests, he was but repeating what he imbibed from Godwin in his early undiscriminating youth.

Mary Wollstonecraft was something quite new in the feminine way. Suffering in youth all the torments of a repressed and restricted woman-child, and possessing a full, passionate nature, she rebelled. Everywhere she turned she saw woman set in an utterly false position, and, as a consequence, silly, affected, degraded. Even those who made a bid for some solid knowledge simpered, and too often, like Mrs Piozzi, repeated by rote, and

in Johnsonian periods, what they did not understand. Mary
never doubted for a moment that woman enfranchised economi-
cally would rise to great things. Unerringly, she detected the
true cause of woman's failure. " It is vain to expect virtue
from women till they are in some degree independent of men."
" Women must have a civil existence in the State." Poor
Mary was terribly alone, and had to work out her new faith in
woman without any human assistance. Fearlessly she exposed
the delicate immorality of Dr Gregory's *Legacy to his
Daughters*, the " most sentimental rant " of Dr George
Fordyce, the oriental despotism of Rousseau ; and not content
with such small game, she entered the lists against the arch-
conservator Edmund Burke, for which Walpole named her
" a hyena in petticoats," and Burke himself reckoned her with
the viragoes and *poissardes*. Mary's wide sympathies were not
only for women. Her knowledge of children had convinced her
that they too had rights, and she had an irresistible faith that
with tyranny put down and political liberty won, the oppressed
peoples of the world would prove themselves capable of the
highest things. And therefore she flung herself into the cause
of the French Revolution, and made that her bone of contention
with Burke.

There is no finer contrast than Fanny Burney for bringing
into relief the special characteristics of Mary Wollstonecraft as a
type of new woman. Fanny welcomed with breathless interest
the French emigrants as they arrived one by one at Juniper
Hall, and listened with horror as Talleyrand, M. d'Arblay,
M. de Narbonne recounted the atrocities of the people. Mary
took a room in Paris and watched their progress through her
window. Fanny was completely overcome at the news of

Louis XVI's martyrdom. Mary watched him go to his death, and would not allow a momentary pity to make her forget the down-trodden poor.

Fanny was a slave to conventions. Mary followed her own nature. Fanny refused to correspond with Madame de Genlis, and asked Queen Charlotte whether she had not done right, and at her father's bidding dropped Madame de Staël, to whom she was attracted. Mary consulted no one about her friendships, and in defiance of legal bonds was willing to be the mother of Charles Imlay's child because she loved him.

Alas! Charles Imlay was faithless ; and when Mary returned to England with little Fanny Imlay, alone and broken in spirit, it was bookseller Johnson who befriended her as he had our lonely Blake. Obviously there was much in common between her and Blake. He was with her in her hope for women, and children, and the poor. She had found herself in spite of mistakes, and her character and her works were informed with vital passion. Had Blake been single, and she drawn into friendship with him, she would have become the perfect type of new woman, imaginative, understanding, impassioned, inspired ; as it happened, it was into Godwin's arms she fell, and not Blake's, and while Godwin took her in like a wandering dove, and gave her shelter and sympathy, yet the slight chill of his marital deportment and reasoned ways would have hindered her, had she lived, from bringing her fine character to full fruition.

Tom Paine presents another type of rebel with whom Blake came into contact. He had already made for himself fast friends and bitter enemies by aiding and abetting the American Rebellion. The thirteen colonies, though irritated by the Stamp Act, were not at once inclined to rebel, and even after Charles Townshend's proposal of tea-duty, South Carolina, Pennsylvania, New York, and Delaware still held back. Paine could wield a powerful pen, and by this means he kept the flame of discontent alive, and urged the States on till Jefferson composed a Declaration of Independence to which the four backward States were brought reluctantly to agree, and on July 4th, 1776, the American United Colonies declared themselves Free and Independent States.

After this success Paine felt that his pen was equal to any task. Having returned to England and fallen in with the Godwin set, he of course shared with them in their sympathies for the French Revolution, and in addition declared himself a deist, and set himself, in his *Age of Reason*, to discredit the Bible. It was all very well when he was doing the rough work of fanning rebellion, but he was ludicrously unfit for the fine work of criticizing the Bible. Its poetry and mysticism and manifold wisdom were not even suspected by him. He stolidly read through the sublime chapters of Isaiah, and thought them worse than the production of a schoolboy ; and when he came to the stories of the Nativity, which, whether fact or poetry, are marvellously beautiful, he became so grossly indecent that one is bound to relegate him to the vulgarest order of Bible-smashers.

His deism was a symptom of the times. Dr Priestley, who also attended Johnson's dinners, was a polished ornament of the sect. They persuaded themselves that God, having set the universe agog, remained Himself wholly outside of it. It was well that Blake should come into personal touch with these rebel deists. They could never appeal to him even for a moment, for he was penetrated all his life with the belief that God dwelt inside of His creation ; and since all theological rebellion tended more and more in the direction of a mechanical deism, he began to suspect that he must look elsewhere to discover the wisdom that should crown his years.

Yet there was something in Paine that appealed to Blake. They were both worshippers of liberty, and while they could not meet on theological ground, they were stirred alike by the portentous and successive crises on the other side of the Channel. Paine felt that he still had work to do. He had served his apprenticeship in America, he would now put forth his whole strength in his *Rights of Man*, and help forward the sacred cause of Liberté, Egalité, Fraternité.

There were other rebels—Holcroft, playwright and translator, friend of Godwin, afterwards to be sent to Newgate ; Hardy and Thelwall ; Horne Tooke, who raised subscriptions for the relief of Americans and spoke of the transactions at Lexington and Concord as " inhuman murders." He was to be tried along with Holcroft and sentenced to twelve months' imprisonment.

Now Blake sympathized with all these rebels in their political aspirations ; but whereas their watchword was reason, and their revolt was in the name of reason, he believed that reason carried one very little way, and that the elemental deeps of life and passion that lie far under reason must be stirred and aroused if the work of rebellion was to bring forth lasting fruit. In any case, the reason-bound men had little to teach him. He had looked to Swedenborg, he had taken knowledge of his advanced contemporaries. Godwin rebelled for political liberty, Mary Wollstonecraft for liberty of women and children, Tom Paine for liberty of man. What was left for Blake ? The sex question had never been dragged out into the light. The subject was unclean. Sexual morality consisted in repression. Nowhere as here does repression breed such poisonous fruits. Was not sex a part of that vital fire and passion in which Blake believed with his whole heart? Was it not true that whatsoever lives is holy? Must not there be liberty for the sexual instinct if it was to be kept clean? For the next ten years Blake became the advocate of bodily liberty, indistinguishable from free-love. This was to be the recurring theme again and again in his prophetic books. This was to be his contribution towards the new kind of man or superman for whom he was groping. Afterwards, when he had given substance and form in his prophecies to the vague and indefinite thoughts that lay in him, he was to learn how to estimate and place them. Not until he had walked the road of mental excess was he to arrive at the palace of wisdom. Once there, he was to revise even his ideas on rebellion.

Keeping these persons and things steadily in view, let us now follow in order and detail the works of Blake's most rebellious period.

As was fitting, Blake sounded the note of rebellion in a poem on the French Revolution.

At this stage—1790–91—the Revolution had not advanced far. The Reign of Terror and the execution of Louis XVI and Marie Antoinette were still in the future. But the Bastille had fallen, and the noise of its fall set the nerves of the overstrung English liberals vibrating. The battle in prose was waged by Paine, Mackintosh, and Mary Wollstonecraft against Burke, and their names came at once into notoriety. Blake was as outspoken, and even more fearless, for he wore publicly the *bonnet rouge* as the outward and visible sign of his faith, but fortunately for him, his natural medium of expression was poetry, and that of a kind hitherto unknown, and so, say what he would, no one paid him the smallest attention. What came doubtlessly as a surprise to himself was that his poem found a publisher; and the first Book, with the promise that the remaining Books of the Poem, which were finished, should be published in their order, was announced to the world by bookseller Johnson in 1791, at the modest price of one shilling.

Blake has a strange allegorical method of dealing with the Revolution which can only irritate those who are not accustomed to his ways. Thus he speaks of the seven dark and sickly towers of the Bastille. To these he gives the descriptive names of Horror, Darkness, Bloody, Religion, Order, Destiny, the Tower of God, and he gives descriptions of the prisoners in the towers corresponding to their names. All these were imprisoned because in some form or other they had bidden for liberty. One was the author of "a writing prophetic"; another, a woman, "refused to be whore to the Minister and with a knife smote him"; another had raised a pulpit in the city of Paris and "taught wonders to darkened souls." The horror of their condition is described with great power, although with too congested an accumulation of baneful images. Thus: "In the tower named Darkness was a man pinioned down to the stone floor, his strong bones scarce covered with sinews; *the iron rings were forged smaller as the flesh decayed.*" That is a Dantesque touch. But when one reads farther down of "an old man, whose white beard covered the stone floor like weeds on margin of the sea, shrivelled up by heat of day and cold of night; his den was short and narrow as a grave dug for a child, with spiders' webs wove and with slime of ancient horrors covered, for snakes and scorpions are his companions," then the piled-up details prevent a clear image, and detract from the value of what has gone before. In contrast to the wretched inhabitants of the Bastille, we are presented with the King and his nobles. Here are names, but no portraits. The King stands for the spirit of kingship in all ages and his nobles are those who uphold "this marble-built heaven," and "all this great starry harvest of six thousand years." They must resist to the death the crooked sickle stretched out over fertile France "till our purple and crimson is faded to russet, and the Kingdoms of earth bound in sheaves, and the ancient forests of chivalry hewn, and the joys of the combat burnt for fuel." (As Blake penned these fine words something of his early Elizabethan passion must have stirred in him.) The King, through whom the spirits of ancient Kings speak, peers through the darkness and clouds, and involuntarily sees the truth : " We are not numbered among the living." Life is with the prisoners who have burst their dens. Let Kings "shivering over their bleached bones hide in the dust ! and plague and wrath and tempest shall cease."

The Archbishop of Paris, symbol of traditional religion, arises and addresses the King. For him revolution can only mean atheism. "God so long worshipped departs as a lamp without oil. . . . The sound of prayer fails from lips of flesh, and the holy hymn from thickened tongues."

Clergy as well as nobles vanish, mitre as well as crown. " The sound of the bell, and voice of the sabbath, and singing of the holy choir is turned into songs of the harlot in day, and cries of the virgin in night. They shall drop at the plough and faint at the harrow, unredeemed, unconfessed, unpardoned ; the priest rot in his surplice by the lawless lover, the holy beside the accursed, the King, frowning in purple, beside the grey plough-man, and their worms embrace together."

This, fine as it is, calls out a still finer speech from Orleans. " Can nobles be bound when the people are free, or God weep when His children are happy ? " Then to the Archbishop he cries : " Go, thou cold recluse, into the fires of another's high flaming rich bosom, and return unconsumed, and write laws. If thou canst not do this, doubt thy theories, learn to consider all men as thy equals, thy brethren, and not as thy foot or thy hand, unless thou first fearest to hurt them."

Finally the voice of the people is heard rising from valley and hill. What though " the husbandman weeps at blights of the fife, and blastings of trumpets consume the souls of mild France, and the pale mother nourishes her child to deadly slaughter," yet when the will of the people is accomplished, then shall the soldier throw down his sword and musket and run and embrace the meek peasant . . . the saw and the hammer, the chisel, the pencil, the pen, and the instruments of heavenly song sound in the wilds once forbidden . . . and the happy earth sing in its course, the mild peaceable nations be opened to heaven, and men walk with their fathers in bliss."

This and much more is what the capture of the Bastille symbolized for Blake. We see that his hopes ran high. The Revolution was to rectify no temporary disorder. It was to set the people free for the first time in the world's history, and so effect a Kingdom of God on earth which had been the passionate yearning of imprisoned souls in all ages. The Kingdom was to come by passion and not intellect, by fire and not snow. And so to cold *doctrinaire* Godwin and such-like, he would have said as Orleans to the Archbishop in the poem : " Go, thou cold recluse, into the fires of another's high flaming rich bosom." Godwin was to go, as we know, into Mary's flaming rich bosom, and to warm as he chilled her ; but even Mary could not bring him to the flaming point which burned in the bosom of William Blake as it had in the bosom of Jesus Christ.

Blake's obscurity protected him from the persecution that was pursuing its victims in the Johnson circle.

On July 14th, 1790, Dr Priestley had arranged a dinner party in Birmingham to commemorate the capture of the Bastille, for which he was mobbed, and his house, containing a fine library, philosophical instruments, and laborious manuscripts, was destroyed. In 1792 Tom Paine was marked out by the Home Office as another victim ; but while he was reporting at Johnson's his public speech of the preceding evening, Blake advised him to decamp at once to France or he was a dead man ; and he, taking the hint, escaped safely to Calais, and was ready to take his part in the National Convention, to which the Department of Calais had appointed him. Paine never returned to England, but he was to encounter many perils during the Reign of Terror, and to write the *Age of Reason*, in which he attacked at once the Bible and French atheism.

Blake, still fired by liberty, wrote his *Song of Liberty* according to Dr Sampson about 1792.

Liberty was the new-born terror, fire, and wonder, brought forth by the eternal Female. Under its inspiration England was to be healed, America renewed, Spain to burst the barriers of old Rome, and Rome herself to cast her keys deep down into eternity. But liberty has a dire conflict with Urizen, here called the jealous King and the gloomy King, who with his grey-browed counsellors, thunderous warriors, curled veterans, and ten commands, makes a fight for life. Liberty stamps the stony law to dust till Empire is no more, and is confident that the lion and wolf shall cease. The sons of liberty are sons of joy, and counting that everything that lives is holy, proceed to act whenever they will.

Thus Blake stumbles again on the vexed subject of sex, and it was to remain something of an obsession with him for many years.

His main thoughts can be gathered from *The Visions of the Daughters of Albion*, which he engraved and printed in 1793. The heroine Oothoon, a Blakean Tess, loves and is beloved by Theotormon. But Bromion, forcibly conveying her to his stormy bed, tears her virgin mantle in twain. Satiated, he cries to Theotormon : " Now thou mayst marry Bromion's harlot, and protect the child of Bromion's rage, that Oothoon shall put forth in nine moons' time."

Theotormon refused. Consumed with jealousy, and reckoning Oothoon a defiled thing, he cannot receive her, and the two, loving, remain apart, consuming their days in misery and tears.

Oothoon calls on Theotormon's eagles to rend away her defiled bosom, that she may reflect the image of Theotormon on her pure transparent breast. The eagles rend their bleeding prey, at which Theotormon, considering that Oothoon suffers what she deserves, severely smiles. She, with no touch of resentment at his self-righteous cruelty, which in truth she is too self-effacing to perceive, reflects the smile, " and as the clear spring, muddied with feet of beasts, grows pure and smiles." It is plain that, whatever her past acts, she is a pure living soul, and Theotormon with his conventional morality is neither clean nor alive. She is " a new-washed lamb tinged with the village smoke," or " a bright swan by the red earth of our immortal river," but she has only to bathe her wings, and she is white and pure to hover round Theotormon's breast.

With the cleansing of her breast comes the clearing of her vision. She is no longer enclosed by her five senses, nor her infinite brain into a narrow circle, but she sees through nature, and comes to see Theotormon as he really is. He was only a selfish devourer. But she cries :

> "Can that be Love, that drinks another as a sponge drinks water,
> That clouds with jealousy his nights, with weepings all the day,
> To spin a web of age around him, grey and hoary and dark ;
> Till his eyes sicken at the fruit that hangs before his sight?"

Then she names it aright :

> "Such is *self-love* that envies all, a creeping skeleton,
> With lamplike eyes watching around the frozen marriage bed !"

Her own love has risen far above such selfishness. She will even lie by his side on a bank, and view him without jealousy as he takes his delight with " girls of mild silver, or of furious gold," and into the heaven of generous love she will bring no selfish blightings. Then with these lovely words she concludes her golden speech :

> "Arise, you little glancing wings, and sing your infant joy !
> Arise, and drink your bliss, for everything that lives is holy."

Here we get in poetry, as later in the *Epipsychidion* of Shelley, a beautiful conception of love and sexual morality. It is what all with any touch of poetical feeling have at times felt since the days of Shelley, and it has appeared in many modern novels and plays. But we must keep in mind that man's deepest feelings and thoughts are revealed by his acts and not his words, however beautiful they may be. Blake was to push his mental liberty to its utmost extent, and advocate a freedom that should satisfy the exorbitant demands of the most modern eroto-maniac; but the fact remains that in his own life he fulfilled to the letter the requirements of traditional morality, not because his wandering fancy was inactive, but because, things being as they are, it is not always possible to translate poetry into act, and the old morality is the only thing that reckons with the disabilities of this tiresome old world.

In this same year Blake wrote and engraved *America, A Prophecy*.

We have already seen his interest in the French Revolution, and his excited hope that it would lead to the regeneration of Europe and the world. He now works backwards to the American War of Independence, and considers that the Demon's (Orc's) light that France received had first been kindled when the thirteen States of North America struck for liberty.

He expected much from America. Believing at this period that rebellion was the direct road to liberty and wisdom, his expectation of America was great because, being farther removed from tradition, her position predisposed her to rebel.

England's boast of colonies was to him a vain boast, and her watchword " Empire " had no magic for him. While the thirteen States of North America were possessions of England, and were ruled by thirteen governors of England's choosing, he believed that America must remain enslaved and unfruitful, and therefore Earth must lose another portion of the Infinite. To lose a portion, however small, of the Infinite is unutterable loss, and so Blake's fiery impetuous sympathies burned towards those men— Washington, Franklin, Paine, Warren—who had stirred the

States to insurrection and revolt. His imagination leapt to an ensuing liberty in which social evils should be left far behind.

" Let the enchainèd soul, shut up in darkness and in sighing,
  Whose face has never seen a smile in thirty weary years,
  Rise and look out ; his chains are loose, his dungeon doors are open ;
  And let his wife and children return from the oppressor's scourge.
  They look behind at every step, and believe it is a dream,
  Singing : ' The sun has left his blackness, and has found a fresher morning,
  And the fair moon rejoices in the clear and cloudless night ;
  For Empire is no more, and now the Lion and Wolf shall cease.' "

Then all the things that religion has repressed spring up and flourish. The pristine fiery joy, once perverted to ten commands, burns through all obstructions, and, as a flame of life, leaps to life, rejoicing in all living things, even in the harlot who remains undefiled, " though ravished in her cradle night and morn." And man walks amidst the lustful fires unconsumed. The fires serve to make his feet " become like brass, his knees and thighs like silver, and his breast and head like gold."

Blake exulted in his vision and proclaimed it in unfaltering tones because he knew that " the soul of sweet delight can never be defiled." Here he adds a touch or two to his vision of sex in *The Vision of the Daughters of Albion*, and he reaches its heart. The *soul* of sweet delight is eternally clean. Once a man has grasped this truth, and it may cost him much mental fight to reach it, then he is able to think and speak cleanly of the passion of love, he can go naked, like Adam in Eden, and the angels of the highest heaven, and know no touch of shame.

There is much in modern literature and art that Blake would have detested, but he would have loved the soul of Sonia the

G

undefiled harlot that Dostoieffski has revealed with such wonderful power in his *Crime and Punishment.*

Blake followed the American conflict until "the British soldiers through the Thirteen States sent up a howl of anguish" and threw their swords and muskets to the earth. They were unable to stand before the flames of Orc ; and since those flames had now reached to France, Blake dreamed that nothing could withstand their hungry course till the regeneration of the world should come.

All this and much more is said in Blake's symbolical way. Here, as in *The French Revolution*, there are no portraits. The rebels of the States, and even Paine, are mere names, and much less real than the angels of the States who carry on the real business. These angels lived in an ancient palace built on the Atlantean hills between America and England. It is interesting to note these things, because the angels of the States are suggested by the angels of the Kingdoms in the apocalyptic book of Daniel, which Blake loved and instinctively understood, and the Atlanteans have always had an irresistible attraction for men of a theosophical turn of mind. Blake was a close student of the apocalyptic books of the Bible all his life ; his knowledge of the Atlanteans probably came to him through his Rosicrucian readings.

America lets us see the profound admiration Blake felt towards Paine for his action in the American War. Later on we shall find him criticizing with some asperity the deism that his friend confessed.

I must pass over Blake's other writings of this year, and merely recount that he again changed his residence, and went to live in Lambeth at 13 Hercules Buildings. Dr Samson says that it is now numbered 23, but authorities cannot agree whether it was this house or the next.

In 1794 Blake engraved his *Europe : A Prophecy*, which is the last of his poems dealing with contemporaneous political events.

Europe stood for Blake in his rebellious mood as the symbol of tradition, authority, science, religion. It was the dead past. " Enitharmon slept eighteen hundred years. Man was a dream, the night of Nature and their harps unstrung." Europe, during this long sleep, was without vision, inspiration, art, and true nature. Her religion, divorced from art, was repressive, and existed by trading on men's fears. Falling under the tyranny of the five senses, she believed only so much as the senses could testify of ; hence she was rational, utilitarian, unimaginative, and joyless. She squinted so abominably with such eyes as she had that she saw nothing as it was. God, man, nature, became creations of man's perverted reason, and God was used as an efficient policeman to keep insurrectionary nations in subjection and vital men in order.

But Blake believed that he had already seen the morning star that heralded the full blaze of the Sun. Already the invisible powers who control nations and men were stirring and preparing for their last fearful conflict, which should result in new heavens and a new earth. The angels were at war. Urizen and his many sons were tightening their sinews for the last life-and-death grip ; against them was Orc, the horrent demon, " already a kindled and quenchless fire, Los, the spirit of inspiration far more nearly allied with fiery passion (Orc) than with cold intellectual reason (Urizen), Los' wife Enitharmon and their many sons and daughters, Rintrah, Palamabron, Elynittria and Ocalythron. These Ossianic and Miltonic principalities and powers were waging huge and terrific war in the heavenly places, and already on earth was kindled in France the earthly counterpart and shadow of the invisible horrible conflict.

The work of regeneration, once begun, could not be arrested. Passion, fire, energy, all the irresistible things pent up in hell, were let loose ; and they would involve Europe and the world in an ocean of blood. The whole cosmos, inward in the heavens, outward in the sun, moon, stars, and earth, was dyed in crimson, until the tribulation such as was not since the world began should work up to the grinding pains of labour, and in infinite pain there should come to the birth the new age of which the prophets and poets had dreamed in all ages.

> " The Sun glow'd fiery red !
> The furious Terrors flew around
> On golden chariots, raging with red wheels, dropping with blood !
> The Lions lash their wrathful tails !
> The Tigers couch upon the prey and suck the ruddy tide ;
> And Enitharmon groans and cries in anguish and dismay.
>
> Then Los arose : his head he reared, in snaky thunders clad ;
> And with a cry that shook all Nature to the utmost pole,
> Called all his sons to the strife of blood."

Blake was very sanguine. He had endured the rude shock of the Reign of Terror, and though he had thrown aside the red cap, he was determined to see in these horrors nothing but the grim accompaniments of every regenerating process. Enitharmon, once awake after her long sleep, would call together the sweet ministers of melodious songs. Ethinthus, Queen of Waters, Manatha-Varcyon on her golden wings, Leutha, soft

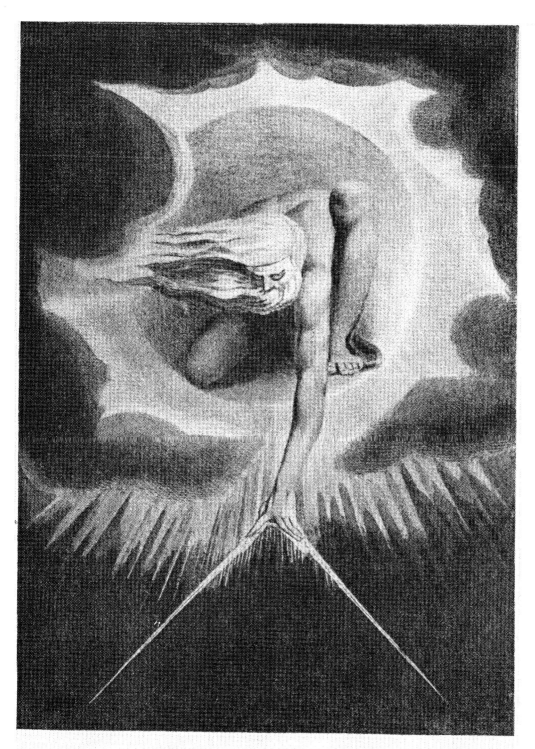

THE ANCIENT OF DAYS.
Frontispiece to Europe.

soul of flowers, Antamon, Prince of the Pearly Dew, " all were forth at sport beneath the solemn moon, waking the stars of Urizen with their immortal songs ; that Nature felt thro' all her pores the enormous revelry, till Morning opened the eastern gates."

Europe has for frontispiece one of Blake's most famous designs—*The Ancient of Days.* The vision was seen against the dark gloom of the upper story of his Lambeth house. Its real ground lay in the Book of Proverbs. Wisdom says : " When He prepared the heavens, I was there : when He set a compass upon the face of the depth . . . then I was by Him, as one brought up with Him."[1]

The author of the Proverbs looks back to the first creation, which God saw to be very good. Blake looks forward to the new. What if all around are dark clouds ? Yet the Ancient of Days is in an orb of light, and He is stooping down and measuring the deep with His compasses. Nothing can stay His hand. The upheaval of Europe, involving the world, is the prelude to the new creation when the Almighty's vision for His universe shall be fulfilled.

Europe touches the limit of Blake's rebellion. During the next thirty years history was to comment on the French Revolution in a way that was not his in his impetuous prophetic books. He was to learn that rebellion is a road to wisdom because it is a species of excess. Excess teaches a man to know what is enough, and when Blake knew the exact value of rebellion he was prepared to read the Past afresh, and find that its treasury contained priceless jewels that he never even suspected while he was passionately searching for some new thing.

[1] Prov. viii. 27–31.

CHAPTER VII

ACTION AND REACTION

In *Europe* Blake reached the boundary of his rebellious mood. The impetus of his rebellion might by its own strength have carried him further down the stream; but the Reign of Terror was a rude check, and among other things it enabled him to climb on to the bank and view the course of events with some degree of detachment.

He found that he could no longer refuse to listen to another voice that had been sounding more or less loudly for some years—the voice of his own experience, and, that which inevitably follows, the voice of the experience of mankind. His thought flew backwards and forwards, backwards to Eden and innocent Adam, followed by the wilderness and the curse, forwards to some more years of travail, and then the crimson dawn glowing on the gathered fruits of experience.

Would experience eventually restore the innocence that was lost with Eden? Were they even things of the same kind? No; Blake was sure that they were contraries, contrary as Swedenborg's heaven and hell, contrary states of the human soul. But many contraries can be married. Innocence married to experience must vanish as innocence, but rise again in a new form in the more fruitful married relation. It appears that with most men innocence lost never returns. Blake never lost his. It is seen in all its infantine simplicity in *The Songs of Innocence*, and it could show itself at any time during his long life. But this divine element is sadly rare even in the poets, and it is its irresistible presence in Blake that makes him wellnigh unique. In ourselves we find from experience knowledge of good and evil, complicated views on philosophy and theology, puzzled brains, and a frightfully murky atmosphere, and it seems Utopian to imagine that it will ever be otherwise.

Blake maintained, and so had the Saints, that when experience had effected its work and disposed of its dirt, smoke, and mud, a glorious something would emerge which innocence could never know, but which will include the innocence that we see in lambs and babies and buttercups and saints. Between what we are and what we shall be is a sandy desert ; and, since Eden is lost, all, even the Christ, have to pass through the desert to gain the promised land. The words of Christ are not the words of one who has lived only in Eden. They are crystalline clear, flaming, simple, deep, and infinitely wise, we should almost say innocent, but as to " create a flower is the labour of ages," so when we look behind the words of Christ, and seize their implications, we discover not only the sorrow and joy, labour and triumph of His own experience, but that of the past labouring ages ; and until we know something of present living experience added to that of the past, we shall never have an inkling of even the simplest words that lie on the face of the gospel.

It was fitting that in 1794, when Blake uttered his prophecy of things to come in *Europe*, he should also gather together his *Songs of Experience*, and engrave them for the joy of posterity.

The Little Girl Lost and *The Little Girl Found* bring together better than any perhaps the two contrary states of innocence and experience.

Lyca, being innocent and only seven summers old, wandered, allured by the wild birds' song. She is lost but not dismayed. Falling asleep, the beasts of prey come around her and minister to her, and finally convey her tenderly to a cave.

Then her parents, experienced but not innocent, arise and seek her. They pass through all the sufferings, sorrows, sighings, of this waste howling wilderness, buying the experience that almost kills them, till in terror they find Lyca among the wild beasts. But beholding Lyca they learn her secret, and

> " To this day they dwell
> In a lonely dell :
> Nor fear the wolfish howl
> Nor the lion's growl."

The Clod and the Pebble give the two contrary states of love. The clod proclaims the love that forgets itself in ministering to others ; the pebble the love that would bind and devour all others, making them contribute to its own delight.

A Poison Tree shows how repressed things secrete poison.

> " I was angry with my friend :
> I told my wrath, my wrath did end.
> I was angry with my foe :
> I told it not, my wrath did grow."

The repressed anger ended in murder. Blake was sure that any passion repressed was equally fatal.

The Schoolboy gives the miserable experience that is thrust upon us all through the blind cruelty of those who would educate us. This experience is so contrary that nothing could be more calculated to crush native innocence, joy, and spring.

> "O ! father and mother, if buds are nipped
> And blossoms blown away,
> And if the tender plants are stripped
> Of their joy in the springing day,
> By sorrow and care's dismay,
> How shall the summer arise in joy,
> Or the summer fruits appear ?
> Or how shall we gather what griefs destroy,
> Or bless the mellowing year,
> When the blasts of winter appear ? "

How indeed ? The question is to parents, schoolmasters, professors, priests. The conditions for young lives are created by those who would strangle life. Yet when experience has been its most contrary, even nailing its victim to a cross, just there is deliverance.

> "Whate'er is born of mortal birth
> Must be consumed with the earth,
> To rise from generation free."

It was Blake's supreme experience that he had been set free from generation. It was by a re-generation, and that had come to him through the death of Jesus.

> "The death of Jesus set me free."

The same year 1794 saw Blake spinning fast the special mythological web with which he was to clothe or strangle his vision. He had separated from all his spiritual teachers ; but Swedenborg lived on in him much more than he owned or even recognized, and Ossian and Milton still governed his imagination. Milton's huge figures were imitated in the mythological figures which were to stalk about his universe to the end ; Ossian's fantastic

names, which always fascinated him, provoked others still more
fantastic. By means of these uncouth dæmons he determined to
set forth his own particular view of the cosmos, which, starting
with eternity, was to fall into creation, and finally, after lightning,
thunder, rolling clouds, and a sea of blood, accompanied by
roarings, shrieks, and howlings, was to attain to salvation by a
return to the divine order.

The " return " is treated of with great fullness in the
Jerusalem : the " fall " is hardly more than sketched in the
fragmentary Books of *Urizen, Los,* and *Ahania.* But as the process of return is the exact reverse to that of the fall, an understanding of the one enables one to fill in the gaps of the other.
If there were other books dealing with the fall more in detail,
I for one can contemplate the loss with equanimity.

The Book of Urizen is supposed to be the account of the creation, and those who endorse this view proceed to identify Urizen
with the Jehovah of the Old Testament, which is as false as to
identify him with the Jesus of the New, although it is only too
true that scores of Christians worship Urizen under the names
of Jehovah and Jesus.

In strict truth, Blake gives no account of the creation at all.
To create can only mean that which the Catholic Church affirms
that it does mean, to make something out of nothing. To
reject this leaves two alternatives—either that God made the
universe out of something outside of Himself, which is dualism,
or out of something inside of Himself, which is pantheism. Blake,
like Swedenborg, adopted the last, but whereas Swedenborg
tried to evade the pantheistic conclusion by his doctrine of discrete
degrees, Blake swam in the pantheistic sea, and was saved from
drowning by clinging to the rocks which he discerned standing

URIZEN IN CHAINS.
From The First Book of Urizen

out in bold outline, and a perception of the ultimate irreconcilable antinomy of good and evil, of sheep and goats, which is a direct contradiction of pantheism, and fits in only with the catholic doctrine. There are other such contradictions in Blake, which did not in the least trouble him. With his passion for contraries he harboured them all, marrying them when he could, and just leaving them when they absolutely refused to unite. He had not the requisite talent for building a coherent system.

What is called, then, Blake's account of the creation is really his account of the fall of the universe out of eternity into time and space, and the consequent appearance of man in his contracted and sense-bound condition. Urizen is the agent in the fall; but he must not be identified with Satan any more than with Jehovah. He, as nearly as possible, represents reason. When he stands in the eternal order working on those things supplied him by Los (imagination), he is a fountain of light, intellect, and joy; when he is rent from Los' side, he becomes self-closed, all repelling, shut up in an abominable void and soul-shuddering vacuum, and his intellect becomes dark and cold because his reason has nothing to work upon except what is supplied by the narrow inlet of the senses.

Thus shut in the deep, he broods until his thoughts take outward shape and form, and there arises " a wide World of solid obstruction." He then proceeds to write his books of wisdom. But his vision being quenched, he is confined to that which his still all-flexible senses provide. He knows much about the terrible monsters that inhabit the bosoms of all—the seven deadly sins of the soul. From his prolonged fightings and conflicts with them there is distilled a kind of wisdom, which he gathers into his books; but it is joyless wisdom, negative rather than positive, restrictive, retributive, censorious, jealous, cruel, penal, and is best solidified in the decalogue with its reiterated " Thou shalt not."

Eternity, which is present and within, rolled wide apart, "leaving ruinous fragments of life." Rent from eternity, Urizen becomes a clod of clay, and Los, beholding him, becomes like him, and is compelled to continue the work of creation in constricted forms. With his hammer he forges links of hours, days, and years. Man with his head, spine, heart, appears; then are formed his eyes, ears, nostrils, throat, tongue, feet— little members that hide from him eternity, and cause him to see the things that are within as though they were without, like the stars of night seen through a great telescope.

After the man the woman appears, whom the Eternal myriads named Pity. She is an emanation from Los, and is named by Blake Enitharmon. Los embraces her, and she begets a child in her own image—a Human Shadow, who is named Orc (passion).

Thus grows up a world of men, women, children, with their various hungers and needs. The Eternals try to provide for these needs by science and religion ; but as they can build their science and religion only from their experience and observation of the contracted universe, the science is sand, and religion a web, and earth's wretched children remain under the cruel rule and curse of Urizen and his sons, calling his laws of Prudence the Eternal Laws of God.

The Song of Los (engraved 1795) adds many interesting particulars of the process by which the world, with its philosophies and religions, has become what it is.

Los, the Eternal Prophet, is the father of all systems of thought, but it does not follow that all are equally true. For Los is out of

LOS.
From The First Book of Urizen.

the divine order, and therefore the systems inspired by him and his many sons, while containing streaks of the eternal truths, are all out of focus.

Thus Rintrah gave Abstract Philosophy to Brahma in the East, and it is defective because it is abstract. The same applies to all modern theosophical revivals of Hindoo religion. An abstraction for Blake was a falling away from concrete reality, and he found his deliverance in the Christian doctrine of God.

Palamabron, another son of Los, gave abstract Law to Trismegistus, Pythagoras, Socrates, and Plato. Abstract Law is also negative, and therefore Orc (passion) finds himself chained down with the chain of Jealousy, and howls in impotent rage.

Sotho teaches Odin a Code of War which at any time may become the philosophy of a nation.

All these, abstract philosophy, abstract law, the Mahometan Bible, Codes of War, with the Churches, Hospitals, Castles, Palaces, which they involve, while seeking to catch the joys of eternity, serve in reality to obliterate and erase eternity altogether, and the children of men schooled in these philosophies behold the vast of Nature shrunk before their shrunken eyes. After the shrinkage there can only arise a philosophy of the five senses, and then Newton and Locke, especially Locke, Rousseau and Voltaire, have it all their own way.

From all this Blake looked for deliverance to the thought-creating fires of Orc, which had flared up in France, and might be expected to spread over Europe, and set even Asia in a conflagration. The Kings of Asia, snug in their ancient woven dens, are startled into self-exertion, and emerging uneasily from their dens, call on kings, priests, counsellors and privy admonishers of men to use their immemorial rights to teach the Mortal Worms, and keep them in the paths of slavery. Happily, Orc's fires are insatiable. Raging in European darkness, he arose like a pillar of fire above the Alps, and, while "milk and blood and glandous wine in rivers rush," led the wild dance on mountain, dale, and plain, till the sullen earth shrunk away, and there dawned the eternal day.

The Book of Los (engraved 1795) begins with the lament of Eno, aged Mother, as she recalls the "Times remote, when love and joy were adoration, and none impure were deemed." For now, alas! Los, who alone could teach joy and liberty, is bound "in a chain and compelled to watch Urizen's shadow." Yet he cannot be bound for ever. Maddened by hard bondage, he rends asunder the vast Solid that has bound him, only to fall through the horrible void of error—"Truth has bounds, Error none "—till his contemplative thoughts arise and throw out some sort of standing-ground amidst the dire vacuity. Urizen by his contemplative thoughts, it will be remembered, had created "a wide World of solid obstruction." Now the two dæmons become rivals, and the grim conflict of the ages is waged incessantly. Los with hammer and tongs organizes lungs (understanding, see Swedenborg), and some Light even appears ; but the book closes with no sign of the ultimate triumph of Los, for Los and Urizen are here rivals: there can be no victory until they cease to be rivals, and re-enter into the union of the eternal order.

The Book of Ahania (engraved 1795) gives the story of Fuzon, Urizen's most fiery son, and therefore the one most obnoxious to his curse. He is mortally wounded by a poisoned rock hurled at his bosom from his father's bow, and his corse is nailed to the topmost stem of the Tree of Mystery, which is religion. Then follows the sad and beautiful lament of Ahania—the wife and emanation of Urizen, and mother of the murdered Fuzon. She recalls, like Eno, the former days, when Urizen stood in the divine order, and she, his lover and wife, joyed in the transports of love, when her heart leaped at the lovely sound of his footsteps, and she kissed the place whereon his bright feet had trod ; when she knew the thrilling joys of motherhood, and nursed her Babes of bliss on her full breasts. These things were now but a memory. Urizen with stern jealous cruelty had put her away, compelling her to walk weeping over rocks and dens, through valleys of death, a shadow upon the void, and on the verge of nonentity, a deep Abyss dividing her from her eternal love. Thus she weeps and laments, wearing a sorrow's crown of sorrows, the remembering happier things.

These short prophetic books, though entirely congenial to the author, were written in a tongue unknown to the public, general or particular. There was every sign that Blake would continue to produce more works, and even on a much larger scale, in this particular kind of composition, and the signs were equally clear that he must look to something else to procure the wherewithal that would enable him and his wife to live.

This something was, of course, engraving, but even the demand for *his* engraving was growing less, and the grim spectre of poverty made his unwelcomed and uncalled-for appearance along with the spectres whom Blake could command. Over this oppressive and grinding spectre he had no command at all.

In 1796 he was asked by Miller, a publisher in Old Bond Street, to make three illustrations to be engraved by Perry for Stanley's English paraphrase of Bürger's *Lenore*. The elements of romance and weird horror in Bürger's work were quite in keeping with a side of Blake's nature that had shown itself in *Elinor*, and so the illustrations were accomplished with marked power and success.

The same year he was engaged on designs for Young's *Night Thoughts*, intended to illustrate a new and expensive edition of what was then considered one of England's great classics. The work was to be published by Edwards, of New Bond Street.

Blake was less free and happy illustrating Young than Bürger. Young has since been slain by George Eliot, but even if she had not killed him, his popularity must have waned in another generation or two. For there was very little healthy human blood in his veins. He was other-worldly, and so was Blake ; but whereas Blake saw in the other world a world of transcendent beauty of which this world was the vegetable mirror, Young saw in it only a reflection of his own particular world. Hence Blake was a mystic, and Young an egotist. Blake forgot himself in the magnificence of eternity, Young's religion was " egotism turned heavenwards."

This is probably the reason why Blake's designs for Young were among the least powerful and interesting things that he did. Give him the Book of Job, or Dante, and he transcends himself, but with Young or Blair to work upon, though he does remarkable work, yet it somehow falls short of his best.

Mr Frederick Shields, who covered the walls of the Chapel of the Ascension with strange pinks and ten thousand hands, has analysed all the more important of Blake's designs, which amounted to five hundred and thirty-seven. Of these only forty-three were published. *The Night Thoughts* was to appear in parts : only one part was published, and Young was handed over to Stothard in 1802 before he was to be, in an elaborate dress, a complete success.

The following year (1797) Blake was at work on *The Four Zoas, or The Death and Judgment of the Ancient Man*. He revised this work a few years later at the time he was planning the *Milton* and *Jerusalem*. I shall have something to say about it when dealing with *Jerusalem*. I will only say just now that the minor prophetic books were preliminary trials to his big flights, and when here, as in *Jerusalem*, a big flight is made, it is found that Blake's mythology has received its completion, and that all the things fermenting in him and striving for utterance do, in these long poems, come to the surface. Anyone who would know him intimately must not be discouraged by their extraordinary appearance, but struggle with them, as with a foreign language, until they yield the last secrets of their mystic author.

H

CHAPTER VIII

WILLIAM HAYLEY

WILLIAM HAYLEY, "the poet," as he delighted to call himself, enjoyed a wide reputation as the author of *The Triumphs of Temper*, which appeared in 1780 and was intended as a poetical and pleasing guide to young ladies how to behave under the provocation of testy fathers and sour aunts, with the promise of a peerless husband if their tempers were triumphant.

For us the poem is pleasantly incongruous and stirs to laughter in the wrong places. The perfect heroine Serena, set down in the midst of artificial society by day, is transported to infernal and supernal regions by night. In the Inferno she sees all the wicked vices in action, and in the Paradise the graces attending on their queen Sensibility. Hayley humbly hoped to emulate Pope's satire in treating of Serena's days, and Dante's sublimities in her nights. He was singularly fortunate in the artists he found to embellish his darling offspring. Stothard and Maria Flaxman, in turn, supplied charming designs, and even Romney was induced to present the divine Emma as Sensibility with her pot of mimosa, to whom Stothard had already done more than justice.

Hayley had been a close student all his life, having mastered Greek and Latin and the more important modern languages. He had read extensively the world's best literature. Taught by Meyer, he had taken up miniature portrait painting till he excelled his master and his eyes failed. He wrote plays which Garrick nearly liked, but which the undiscerning public never liked at all. He reckoned himself not merely a connoisseur in art, music, architecture, and sculpture, but also as one who might have distinguished himself in any one of these difficult arts had envious time permitted. Confident that Heaven had bestowed on him her best gift of poetry, he felt it his duty to renounce his opportunity to excel in so many arts and devote himself to that which all discerning people acknowledged to be the highest.

The Triumphs of Temper was his first great success, and the many highly flattering things said to him by artists and famous literary men confirmed him in the faith, though he had never really doubted, that he was a man of genius. That was the opinion of elegant Mrs Opie, feeling Anna Seward, diffident Romney, copious Hannah More, and portentously learned Edward Gibbon. Yet time has been pitiless with the bard of Sussex, and instead of discovering a steady or even a flickering light shining in the gross darkness of his times, we of the twentieth century can see in him, if we take the trouble to see at all, nothing but an amusingly solemn specimen of a male Blue-stocking.

With so assured a position and never a shadow of self-doubt, he was able to live with himself on most cordial terms of good temper and serenity, and, like others of his type, extend his self-esteem to his fellows, particularly if they were publicly admired. To these he generally effected an acquaintance by a polite little letter of self-introduction.

His most important catch was Romney, to whom he was introduced by Meyer in the autumn of 1776. Hayley possessed accidental advantages over Romney in good birth and education. Romney was sufficiently impressed through self-conscious lack of these, and when in addition he found that his diffidence was met by Hayley's confidence, his depression by serenity, he allowed him to gain that ascendancy over him which was out of all proportion to his intrinsic merit, and which has irritated all biographers of the artist against the poet. Yet if Hayley contrived to get possession of Romney and his pictures, he also helped him for a considerable time to fight against his melancholy. Let us in fairness remember that.

Another important friend was Cowper, whom Hayley caught considerably later in life. Visits were exchanged, and Hayley set himself with much good will to combat the ghastly melancholia that was getting its death-grip on him. After Cowper's death there was some friendly wrangling between Hayley and Lady Hesbeth about who should write his Life. Hayley was easily persuaded to undertake it, and by its accomplishment won for himself a latter rain of gratifying applause just when his popularity seemed to be on the decline.

Hayley lived till 1820, which was actually long enough to outlive his public. His *Life of Romney* was not a success. He and his works would have died together but for his unfortunate habit of fastening himself on to great men. His cancerian grip of them has given him vicarious immortality, and made him obnoxious to the kicks of those who write the lives of Romney, or Cowper, or Blake.

The particular friend of Hayley who most concerns us here was Flaxman. He introduced Blake to Hayley from motives of pure kindness, knowing Blake's struggle to live, and believing that Hayley was just the man to help him.

Flaxman had drawn Hayley's attention to Blake in a letter written as early as 1784, in which he quotes Romney as saying that Blake's historical drawings rank with those of Michael Angelo. But not until 1800 did the two men meet. Early in that year—May 6th—Blake wrote to Hayley to condole with him on the loss of his son Thomas Alphonso, who had been studying sculpture with Flaxman. By September it was settled that Mr and Mrs Blake should leave Lambeth and go and settle at Felpham, where Blake would be only a stone's-throw from Hayley, and ready to help him in his poetical and biographical works by engraving for them suitable designs.

Blake was destined to stay three years at Felpham, and he always regarded this period as marking a most important crisis in his life. Since the publication of his *Poetical Sketches* in 1783 he was conscious of being under a cloud. His visions that had been so bright and inspired him to songs of such divine simplicity had not vanished, but they had lost their crystalline clearness. His cloudy vision appeared in uncertain art. It is true that his allegiance to the linear schools never wavered, and Michael Angelo remained the supreme master in his eyes, but for a time he was fascinated by the luscious ornament and colour of the Venetian school, and with his passion for uniting contraries believed that he might marry Florence and Venice. The same uncertainty appeared in his spiritual life. We have followed him through various stages of rebellion, and seen how his faith in rebellion received a rude shock from the Reign of Terror. Since then he was learning more and more to explore the riches of the past, but he had not gone far enough to place his rebellion and to see it and that of his rebel contemporaries in its proper historical perspective. He was disturbed also by a restless ambition of worldly success.

Many men whose gifts were much inferior to his own were famous and rich. Sir Joshua did all that a spiritually blind man could do, and was reckoned with the giants. Romney, whose art Blake much preferred to Reynolds's (he was decidedly of the Romney faction), on account of its greater simplicity and more scrupulous regard to outline, was sufficiently famous and remunerated ; but Blake, whose gifts were rarer than any, had scant recognition and scant money, and he still hoped that with an influential patron he might take his place in contemporary fame, and incidentally make enough money to relieve him of all anxiety for the future. For he was being ground by poverty. His wants were simple enough—food, clothing, materials of work—but when the supply falls even a little below the want, then the grinding process begins and carries on its inexorable work until the spirit breaks. But now friend Flaxman had introduced him to poet Hayley, who was not only famous for his literary work, but also for a remarkable and untiring zeal in the service of those he reckoned his friends.

Blake's hopes rose high, and his spirits overflowed. He wrote an enthusiastic letter to Flaxman attributing to him all his present happiness, and enclosing lines in which he recalls his successive friends " in the heavens "—Milton, Ezra, Isaiah, Shakespeare, Paracelsus, Boehme—and concludes by affirming that he has seen such visions of the American War and the French Revolution that he " could not subsist on the earth, but by conjunction with Flaxman, who knows to forgive nervous fear." Flaxman had studied Swedenborg, and could perfectly understand such language.

On September 21st, 1800, Sunday morning, he writes to the " dear Sculptor of Eternity " that he has arrived at their cottage with Mrs Blake and his sister Catherine, and that Mr Hayley has received them with his usual brotherly affection.

He found Felpham " a sweet place for study." The quiet, cleanness, sweetness, and spiritual atmosphere of the place stirred his cosmic consciousness and gave him quick access to the great memory reaching back far beyond his mortal life, and enabled him to recall his works in eternity that were yet to be produced in time.

And Hayley was excessively kind. Still under a cloud, shaken in self-confidence, Blake's consequent diffidence united with his instinctive trust of men, and for a month he believed that Hayley was a prince.

Hayley was busy decorating his " marine villa," to which he had lately come from Eartham. Flaxman had already been drawn in to help, much as Mrs Mathew had used him at an earlier date ; and now Blake was bidden to paint a set of heads of the poets which were to form a frieze to Hayley's library Hayley was at work on some ballads, *Little Tom the Sailor* and others, to which Blake was to contribute designs. *Little Tom* was for the benefit of a Widow Spicer at Folkestone and her orphans, as Blake understood, and also for the emolument of Blake, as we learn from a letter of Hayley's to the Reverend John Johnson.

Hayley always loved to teach his friends. He had been anxious to improve Romney's epistolary style ; and now it occurred to him that he might teach Blake miniature portrait painting. As usual, his purpose was thoroughly kind. He did not think that Blake's work had much marketable value ; but he believed that if he proved an apt pupil he could procure him plenty of sitters from among his neighbours who would pay well, and thus Blake would become a real success.

In this Hayley showed himself a wise child of this world, but hardly a child of light. Blake's genius did not lie in drawing portraits. A face for him immediately became a symbol, and lost its time traits as it gained in eternal significance. It is often said that Enitharmon was Mrs Blake ; but if this were so, she was Mrs Blake as no one but Blake could ever see her. In reality he possessed the faculty which was pre-eminent in the authors of the Book of Genesis and St John's Gospel. As the characters of Abraham, Isaac, and Jacob, of Peter, James, and John were seen and portrayed in an eternal light, so likewise Blake would have striven to present his opulent sitters, but the result would not have been that for which they would have been willing to pay their money.

Blake took kindly and without question to the new task. " Miniature," he says, " has become a goddess in my eyes. . . . I have a great many orders, and they multiply." Hayley was glowing with satisfaction. But Blake, in one little month, after repeated efforts of self-deception, could no longer hide from himself that he saw Hayley as he really was. He was learned, of course, and genteel, and kind, and admired with gush what it was correct to admire. But of insight there was none. He was born under a watery sign and not a fiery. He was really a crab ambling around his enclosed garden with his lame leg, and getting his claws into the tender skin of those who, he had been told, were really men of fire.

Blake's disappointment was bitter. His patron was blind to his real genius, to which he must at all costs be faithful. Hayley was, and continued to be, very much a corporeal friend, but he was a spiritual enemy. Blake's fond hopes were dashed. He tottered on the verge of a horror of great darkness, and escaped the darkness only by falling into a mild and pleasant slumber, lulled by Hayley's amazing amiability, mildness, and crooning serenity. From this slumber he might—who knows?—never have awakened, but for the discernment of his real friends—Flaxman and Butts—whose faith finally aroused him and drew him away from the enchanted ground.

But though he saw, he said nothing. His spiritual friends (on the other side) commanded him "to bear all and be silent, and to go through all without murmuring, and, in fine, hope, till his three years shall be accomplished." When Hayley was more than usually exasperating, Blake vented himself in an epigram, and, much relieved, went on quietly.

Thus, when Blake was convinced that Providence did not mean him to paint miniatures, he wrote:

"When Hayley finds out what you cannot do,
  That is the very thing he'll set you to do."

Again, Blake discovered that Hayley's virtues and faults were both of the feminine order. It was a feminine instinct that had prompted him to write *The Triumphs of Temper* and the *Essay on Old Maids*. A brilliant epigram of Blake's accounts for this odd psychic twist, and flashes Hayley before us:

"Of Hayley's birth this was the happy lot:
  His mother on his father him begot."

That was the true state of affairs. But Blake obeyed his spiritual friends, and for a long time no sign appeared in his letters that there was anything the matter.

Hayley was also anxious to teach Blake Greek. Like most men of his times, he believed that no man could attain to the highest degree of excellence who had not mastered Greek and Latin. He probably thought that a knowledge of Greek would at least correct some of Blake's vagaries. Blake was quick at languages, and soon Hayley was able to write to Johnson : " Blake is just become a Grecian, and literally learning the language. . . . The new Grecian greets you affectionately."

Blake, however, never attained to his teacher's proficiency ; he learnt just enough to be able to formulate to himself the nature of the Greek genius, and to see it in relation to his own. " The Muses were the Daughters of Memory." The inspiration of the Bible was from a higher source than Memory. Memory is the indelible record of experience. Inspiration is always a breaking into experience to the creation of something new. Then only is the new creation handed over to Memory. Thus Inspiration feeds Memory, but is not its fruit. Imagination is the true instrument of Inspiration. When Blake saw all this clearly, he wrote in the Preface to *Milton* : " We do not want either Greek or Roman Models if we are just and true to our own Imaginations." Greek and Latin have their abiding place in Memory, and Blake was about to write fine things about Memory, which he calls the Halls of Los ; but for himself they did not stimulate his imagination. To master them would add to his culture ; but mere culture is always barren.

Hayley's last attempt to teach Blake was in March 1805, the month in which Klopstock died. He translated parts of Klopstock's *Messiah* aloud for Blake's benefit. Certain lines by Blake with big gaps have been preserved, which are hard for us to understand. The only thing we are quite sure about them is that they were written " after *too much* Klopstock."

There was one great name that held Hayley and Blake alike at this time. We know that Blake had always admired Milton's superb gifts, while he disliked his theology. Blake's special friends had also been preoccupied with Milton. Fuseli, for example, not only disagreed with Dr Johnson's strictures on the poet, but he had been inspired by his ardent imagination to paint a series of pictures illustrating the poet's works, and these had been on public view at a Milton Gallery opened on May 20th, 1799, and reopened March 21st, 1800.

While Blake was with Hayley he naturally heard much of Milton from his latest biographer ; and again their united interest in Cowper led them back to Milton, because of Cowper's cherished desire to edit Milton, with notes and translations.

In 1790, when Boydell's Shakespeare Gallery was a success, " bookseller " Johnson was fired with the idea of bringing out a magnificent Milton Gallery, " surpassing any work that had appeared in England." It was to contain Cowper's notes and translations and Fuseli's illustrations, for which the best engravers were to be found. The services of Sharpe and Bartolozzi were enlisted, and Blake was asked to engrave *Adam and Eve observed by Satan*. The project fell through owing to Cowper's mental indisposition ; but when Hayley was engaged on the *Life of Cowper* and Blake on its engravings, Cowper's *Milton* came uppermost again in their minds, and it occurred to Hayley that it would be a good plan to bring out a fine edition of the delayed work, with engravings after designs by Romney, Flaxman, and Blake. The profits of the work were " to be appropriated to erect a monument to the memory of Cowper in St Paul's or Westminster Abbey." To this work was to be added Hayley's

Life of Milton, so that the whole necessarily would spread out to three quarto volumes. The project was abandoned. Instead of the three volumes, one volume with Cowper's notes finally appeared in 1808, and instead of the proceeds going to a monument in St Paul's, they were given for the emolument of an orphan godson of the Sussex Bard.

Thus Blake's thought and time were fully occupied. Besides the designs for Hayley's ballads, engravings were required for the Cowper *Life*. Butts was to be kept supplied with a fresh picture as fast as Blake could paint it ; and his own more secret thought was ruminating over Milton, and his stay at Felpham, and his dreams for the future. These were to take form in his longest poetical works—*Milton*, *The Four Zoas*, and *Jerusalem* ; but as they are of extreme importance for understanding Blake, they must be kept over to another chapter.

Blake was thoroughly interested in this work, for he admired Cowper, and considered that his letters were " the very best letters that were ever published." It is necessary to remember his reverence for Cowper, as also for Wesley and Whitefield, because in the poems there are many vigorous attacks made on religion, and some of Blake's modern imitators follow him in the attack. The moderns for the most part are irreligious, but Blake professed to love true religion and true science. What he hated above all things was religion divorced from life and art. Such religion becomes very intense, as in the Pharisees, and when great decisions are called for, as in the trial of Christ, it invariably utters its voice on the wrong side.

Blake's engravings for the Cowper *Life* were after designs by other artists, the most important being the head of Cowper by Romney. To engrave after another is irksome, and there

MIRTH AND HER COMPANIONS.

was further irritation when he found that Hayley was as ready to instruct him how to engrave as to paint miniatures.

Since Hayley could never disguise his inmost thoughts, Blake soon perceived that he intended to keep him strictly to the graver, as he had no opinion of his original works, whether in poetry or design. Blake found relief in painting for Thomas Butts, who was his friend and patron for over thirty years, and to whom he sent exquisite pictures, and some letters priceless for their revelation of the writer.

From these we learn the nature of Blake's spiritual crisis at Felpham.

Miniature portrait painting drove home to him the vast difference between historical designing and portrait painting. Portrait requires nature before the painter's eye, historical designing depends on imagination. Nature and imagination were as antithetical in Blake's eye as nature and grace in the theologian's, and just here he kept as far away from pantheism as he could in his obstinate determination to keep nature and imagination as separate as the sheep and the goats. While agreeing with Blake in keeping them apart, I suppose most of us would say that the finest portrait painting depended on imagination no less than historical designing.

The atmosphere of Felpham induced in Blake long fits of abstraction and brooding, and he pushed his thoughts on miniature forwards to the recollecting of all his scattered thoughts on art. He determined to discontinue all attempts at eclecticism. Venetian *finesse* and Flemish *picturesque* were " excellencies of an inferior order " and " incompatible with the grand style." He was convinced that the reverse of this—uniformity of colour and long continuation of lines—produces grandeur. So said

Sir Joshua, who did not always practise what he preached in his discourses ; so said Michael Angelo, whose profession and practice were one ; so said Blake, who was decided, while adhering to the principles of the great Florentine, to be true to his own genius, so that his work should be as distinct from Michael Angelo's as Caracci's from Correggio's, or Correggio's from Raphael's.

Here was strength for Blake in knowing his own mind about his art and methods, and following it. It helped him out of his paralysing diffidence, which Hayley fostered, and made more clear the real issue between him and his patron. He strove to see the situation in the largest light possible. The old question of God's providence exercised him. Did God bring him to Felpham ? Did God keep him there ? If so, it must be because it was not fit for him at present to be employed in greater things. That thought kept him patient. When it is proper his talents will be properly exercised in public. But God guides by cleansing man's understanding and pushing him forwards to a decision. He understood his art, yet Hayley objected to his doing anything but the mere drudgery of business. He trusted his art, and he saw how he must work. Let him trust himself, and then ? He saw all clearly now, as he had seen it in the first month, although he had stifled his apprehensions. God had given him a great talent. It would be affected humility to deny it. If he stayed with Hayley he would paint miniatures, make money, and make his beloved Kate comfortable for life ; but he would sell his divine birthright. If he obeyed God by following the gifts He had bestowed on him, then farewell to Hayley and lovely Felpham : he must return without delay to London, and once more he and Kate together must face the grinding life of poverty. Anyone who knows Blake must know what decision he would make. He made it silently, irrevocably. By the beginning of October 1803 he and Kate were back again in London, lodging in South Molton Street, with a sense of escape and liberty which more than compensated for the uncertain prospect of the future.

Blake had not quite finished with Felpham. Before leaving he had had a disagreeable affair with a private in Captain Leathe's troop of 1st or Royal Dragoons. From a letter of Blake's to Mr Butts, dated August 16th, 1803, we learn that this man was found by him in the garden, invited to assist by the gardener without his knowledge. He desired him politely to go away ; and on his refusal, again repeated his request. The man then threatened to knock out his eyes, and made some contemptuous remarks about his person. Blake thereupon, his pride being affronted, took the man by the elbows and pushed him before him down the road for about fifty yards. In revenge, the soldier charged Blake with uttering sedition and damning the King. Blake had no difficulties in gathering witnesses for his defence. He was summoned before a bench of justices at Chichester and forced to find bail. Hayley kindly came forward with £50, Mr Seagrave, printer at Chichester, and protégé of Hayley's, with another £50, and himself bound in £100 for his appearance at the Quarter Sessions after Michaelmas. The trial came off at Chichester on January 11th, 1804. The Duke of Richmond presided as magistrate. Hayley had procured for the defence Samuel Rose (Cowper's friend), and between them they had no difficulty in releasing Blake.

There would have been no need to repeat this story, except that the event made a deep impression on Blake. Skofield, the soldier's name, became in his mind an abiding symbol, and the soldier's contempt for his person decided him to change his deportment.

Blake's humble birth and childlike trust of his fellows had united to produce in him a too passive and docile manner. There was plenty of fire within, and the lamb knew how to roar ; but he judged that his roar need not be provoked if his appearance somehow warded people off from taking a liberty with him. Diffidence is not a virtue. Blake's too passive deportment changed as he gradually became more self-confident. Hence the Skofield episode left a lasting mark on both his mind and body.

Blake's decisive step in leaving Hayley and following his own will immediately preceded the noonday glory of his genius. Hayley must have thought that Blake was extremely ungrateful after the invariable kindness that he had shown him ; and if Hayley liked to call his neighbouring friends around him and put his case to them, probably all, without a single dissentient voice, would have agreed that he had shown himself a Christian and a gentleman, and that charity itself could not demand of him to trouble himself any further about such a crazed visionary as Blake. Blake not only thought otherwise, but turning to the Gospel as he was wont to do, he found a word of Christ that convinced him that Christ was on his side. " He who is not with me is against me." There were a thousand evidences that Hayley was not with the real Blake that was striving to manifest himself in time, and therefore he was against him, and an enemy to his genius. Blake went to Felpham shaken in himself and diffident. When there is diffidence (dispersal of faith) there is a lamentable waste of precious energy. Blake left Felpham reassured that the light he had seen in his youth was the true light, and confident (confidence is concentration of faith) that if he remained faithful to his real self, he would also be found on the side of Christ, and that this true self-confidence must result in beautiful work of the creative order. That was the supreme hour in his life. The full vision must come. Like Habakkuk, he was on his tower, assured that though it tarry it would come and not tarry. He was not impatient. " The just shall live by his faith." Blake had faith, and he asked no more ; but he gained a thousandfold more, and the full vision came to him in a way that must seem odd to a child of the world, but wonderfully appropriate to one who understands what is the nature of the fire that sustains and consumes the artist's soul.

During the months of 1803–4 a certain Count Truchsess, who owned a valuable collection of pictures, exhibited them at a gallery in the New Road, opposite Portland Place, London. The pictures were by German, Dutch, Flemish, Italian, Spanish, and French masters. The masters included Albert Dürer, Hans Holbein senior, Breughel, Vandyck, Michael Angelo, Leonardo da Vinci, Bourdon, Watteau.

Blake went to see the pictures, and must have been unusually excited and thrilled at seeing works by Michael Angelo and Albert Dürer directly, and not through the blurred medium of poor engravings. The divine frenzy stirred in his soul. The next day, suddenly, he was enlightened with the light he enjoyed in his youth. The cloud that had hung over him for twenty years vanished, the grim spectre (reason) who had haunted his ways and checked his inspiration fled with the cloud. Blake was drunk with intellectual vision, and in his drunken hilarity came to himself, knew what was his proper work, and once for all gave himself with passionate surrender to that which his whole and undivided being saw to be good.

It will take us the rest of our time gathering some of the fruits of Blake's richly matured genius.

I

Blake wrote an enthusiastic account of his mystic experience to Hayley, of all men—Hayley who had so exasperated him, and made him sore, and, in his soreness, say biting things. Now he was thoroughly at peace with himself, and could regard Hayley with the kindness and tolerance that before had been impossible. For a while he continued to correspond with him while he was occupied with his *Life of Romney*. Blake engraved a portrait of the artist for the frontispiece which never appeared, and a fine engraving of Romney's *Shipwreck*, which appeared along with the other engravings by Caroline Watson. The *Life of Romney* was a dreary performance. Like the *Life of Cowper*, it revealed its subject only when it gave his letters. For the rest, it abounds in a welter of elegant eighteenth-century words and phrases which assure us that " the poet " never saw even Romney and Cowper as they really were, and therefore it is not surprising that he saw in Blake merely a mild and harmless visionary who might do paying work if only he would listen to the wise counsel that he was always ready to give.

Peace be with Hayley! Among those that appear before Peter's Gate, we cannot help thinking that he will be more readily admitted than the vast crowd of eighteenth-century squires who will knock at the gate, and stamp and fume if it is not opened to them on the instant.

CHAPTER IX

THE BIG PROPHETIC BOOKS

BLAKE'S "three years' slumber," as he called it, hypnotized, I presume, by Hayley's lulling kindness, were amongst the most important in his life. If he slumbered, yet his dreams were unusually active ; and, since feelings are more intense in dreams than when wide-awake, it is not surprising that Blake's inner life was in a violent commotion. Any stirring of his feeling immediately set his supersensual faculty vigorously to work. Visible persons and things were tracked back to invisible principalities and powers, his cosmic consciousness quickened, the need to create possessed him, and he found relief only in giving rhythmic expression to his spiritual reading of mundane things.

This was the mental process that we saw at work in his *French Revolution* and *America*. Now it was moving among the persons and things connected with his own life; but it is not less important, for the same mighty agencies govern individuals and nations alike, and link them up together, so that they are interchangeable manifestations of eternal laws and states.

The practical outcome was *Milton*, *Jerusalem*, and a revision of *The Four Zoas*, begun some time about 1795. These claim our close attention, for they contain, for those who have patience to probe their forbidding exterior, the treasure of one who had run the road of excess, not of profligacy but rebellion, and now reached the palace of wisdom.

131

On April 25th, 1803, Blake wrote to Thomas Butts : " I have written this poem (*Milton*) from immediate dictation." Later in the same year (July 6th), he writes : " I can praise it, since I dare not pretend to be any other than the secretary ; the authors are in Eternity. I consider it the grandest Poem that this world contains. Allegory addressed to the intellectual powers, while it is altogether hidden from the corporeal understanding, is my definition of the most sublime Poetry." In the Preface to *Milton* Blake asserts, in effect, that Shakespeare and Milton were shackled by the Daughters of Memory, who must become the Daughters of Inspiration before work of the highest creative order can be produced. Here he regards Memory as a hindrance, and comparing the Preface with the above quotations, we learn that he strove to put Memory aside while the authors in Eternity were dictating to him.

But in the *Jerusalem* there are, scattered throughout, references to what he calls the Halls of Los, familiar to readers of mystical literature as the Akashic or Etheric records, and called by Yeats the great Memory.

" All things acted on Earth are seen in the bright Sculptures of Los's Halls, and every Age renews its powers from these Works." [1]

Here Memory serves to renew an age, and then becomes the recipient of the age's inspired works.

These passages, taken together, open up again the great questions of Inspiration, Memory, Creation, Mechanism, and since each one of these words is now made to stand for differing conceptions, they are ambiguous, and we may not use them without first defining sharply what we mean. We speak of the true

[1] *Jerusalem*, 15. 61–69.

poet like Shakespeare, the true mystic like Blake, the true saint like Catherine of Siena, and the true Book like the Bible as all being inspired, yet in each case the inspiration is of a different order. The common element which justifies the one word is originality. Shakespeare's inspiration depends on the great Memory, on his own complex nature, and his consuming spirit of observation; but at the moment of his inspiration, all these things seem in abeyance, and the words well up as if a spirit not himself had given them to him. His originality consists in the unique impression that his rich understanding gives of the elements supplied by the Past and Present, but not in the creation of a new element. The same may be said of Dante, Milton, Shelley.

The inspiration of the Bible contains all these elements, which constitute its purely human side, but there is something else which has given it its supreme power in all ages. The writers of the Bible remember and observe and think, but they also utter themselves as they are moved by the Holy Ghost. It is this last mysterious happening that inspires the creative element. The inspired poet has aided his observation and experience by drawing on the great Memory, the inspired Bible has added to the great Memory something that was not in it before. The poet can renew us, yet keeps us within the circle of the cosmic consciousness. The Bible can inspire us and lift us out of the circle far above the seven heavens of the cosmos. And that is our rescue from that nightmare of eternal recurrence which set Nietzsche's fine brain tottering down to its foundations.

The inspiration of the poet is general, and that of the Bible unique ; but there still remains a special kind to which Blake, like many other mystics, laid claim.

When Blake was perplexed at Felpham, he referred to his spiritual guides, who were in their turn subject to God. They, according to him, were the real authors and inspirers of his prophetic books. This sort of language was rare in the eighteenth century, but is quite familiar to readers of theosophical books, ancient or modern.

They teach that there are seven planes of consciousness from the physical to the mahaparanirvanic, which together make up the cosmos. The two highest planes are beyond the reach of human conception ; but there are not a few to-day who claim to have attained to the fifth nirvanic plane. Here the consciousness is so finely developed, and its vibrations respond so readily, that the subject comes into touch with other intelligences, and often submits to them entirely for guidance.

In St Paul's day this teaching was familiar at Ephesus in the form of gnosticism. He did not disbelieve in the reality of the seven planes, but he disagreed with the gnostics in their blind faith in the trustworthiness of the guides. He believed that many of them were so evil that when Christians became conscious of them, they needed the whole armour of God to protect them against their wiles. Here is the difference between the Christian and pantheistic teaching. The pantheist thinks that because a thing is spiritual it is therefore holy and good ; Christianity believes in fallen spiritual beings. The pantheist believes that to reach the nirvanic plane is to attain to holiness ; Christianity says that all the planes of the cosmos are tainted, and if one reached even the seventh, one would still have need of cleansing. Theosophy keeps one for ever within the cosmic circle ; Christianity lifts one beyond the circle into the ascended Christ, and teaches that one is safe on the different subtle planes of consciousness only while one abides in Him. Doubtless there are good guides, but the danger is great because it is so difficult to try the spirits.

Blake here as elsewhere wavers between the two views. With certain reservations he dips on the Christian side. He travels round the cosmos, but in a spiral ; and the top of his spiral—his Jacob's Ladder—reaches not to the seventh plane but to the Throne of God, which is far above the charmed circle. Hence man is able to climb beyond the defiled cosmos into the pure heaven of God. That is his redemption.

Blake's vision, then, ranging freely among the planes of consciousness, gives him access to the great Memory which is within the cosmos ; and at rare moments he goes beyond the cosmos, and then his words proceed from the highest inspiration.

In appraising the value of Blake's defamation of the Greeks' inspiration, one must remember that he was not a profound Grecian. His studies with Hayley cannot have carried him into the heart of the Greek genius. When he limits its inspiration to Memory, there is no scholar, I imagine, that would agree with him. The Greeks did make an invaluable contribution to the world's memory ; and while one source of their inspiration came from the past, we must further admit that it was the past wedded to the present which actually produced something new, that is, of the creative order.

Blake's own inspiration when it came from his spiritual guides is not of such a high order as the Greek's at his highest. The so-called guides, if we may trust St Paul, are inside of the cosmos, like the great Memory, and their source of wisdom is from this world, which is the arena of the Church in her militant course.

It is only by watching her that they are able to get glimpses of the manifold wisdom of God. Hence to place oneself under their guidance is a hindrance to receiving that highest inspiration that comes direct from the Spirit of God.

Blake was wrong, too, in his efforts to shut off Memory. Of course he could not succeed. Every page of *Jerusalem* shows that Memory was at work though shackled. Memory alone could have made it coherent and a luminous whole, as it had made *Paradise Lost;* but it was not free enough to keep its different scenes, often very beautiful, from flying far apart, and the imagination grows weary in trying to capture the complete picture.

The one thing in these poems that we can positively affirm to be new is their symbolism, and that cannot be defended. Symbolism is beautiful only as it is universal, or can become so. It should be one language against many tongues. But Blake's is not even the tongue of a nation or a tribe. It is his own private invention, and, incidentally, uncouth, forbidding, unintelligible, and in actual fact a little insane. It is true that we can learn his symbolism after much labour ; but a beautiful and catholic symbolism is the one thing that we have a right to understand, without learning, through the imagination, which Blake always affirmed to be divine.

Blake could not afford to indulge these idiosyncrasies. Like all mystics, he found it difficult to adjust the inner things that were real to him to the outer that were but a shadow. Since most people find the outer things are the substantial reality, they are not only moving in a different world from that of the mystic, but they are puzzled to know when the letter of his statements is to be taken.

Ezekiel says that he ate his meat baked with cow's dung ; Blake, that Hayley, when he could not act upon his wife, hired a villain to bereave his life. We know sufficient of Blake's relation to Hayley to understand that Hayley's murderous purpose was towards Blake's spiritual life, not his corporeal, and that he tried to prevail on Blake through his wife. We may hope also that Ezekiel did not really eat "abominable flesh," or lie for a preposterously long time on his left side. We mention the mystic's hazy treatment of external actions, to explain Blake ; but we hope the mystic of the future will be more considerate of what his words are likely to convey to others, and then clear them of all ambiguity.

Blake should have guarded himself perpetually here, but was too proud or wilful to do so. Hence with his merging of inward and outward things, and using the same language for both, added to his private symbolism, what should have been his greatest poems have become submerged continents in which you may discover endless treasures only if you dare to dive, and can hold your breath under water.

Let us dive for the sake of understanding the growth of Blake's mind.

I will take *Milton* separately, and *The Four Zoas* and *Jerusalem* together.

Blake's feelings towards Milton had always been divided. He saw in him the highest order of poetic genius, but also, ominously present, the spirit of reason (Urizen) enthroned in the wrong place, and a servile love of the classics that placed him under the heel of the Daughters of Memory. To change the metaphor, Milton's Pegasus was ridden by Urizen.

Blake's final criticism of Swedenborg was that he drew the

line in the wrong place between heaven and hell ; and his amend-
ment was to take his two contraries and marry them. From
that time forward his first question in trying a man's religion was,
Where do you draw the line ? Popular religion always draws
it in the wrong place. Good things are reckoned evil and evil
things good. But as Blake continued to put his question to the
world's great spirits, he counted twenty-seven different answers
that had produced twenty-seven different churches, each church
having its own particular heaven and corresponding hell. He
had hoped to unite all these contraries as successfully as he had
Swedenborg's ; but when he came to Christ's division, finding
that nothing would unite His sheep and goats, and His wheat
and tares, he henceforth took Christ's dividing line as absolute, and
the line of any other as right only when it coincided with Christ's.

Applying this test to Milton, Blake saw that he wrongly
divided heaven and hell, and that this fatal mistake necessarily
affected the characters of his Messiah and Satan. Messiah,
who should have stood for the supreme poetic genius, was the
embodiment of restrictive reason, and Satan, who by immemorial
tradition is absolute evil, was endowed with a marvellous imagination that inevitably brought with it certain virtues. When Blake
inquired for the root cause of this perversion in Milton, he
traced it to the fact that Reason had largely usurped the place
of Imagination. He then took one more customary step.
He set Milton in his imagination in the light of the eternal
order. Seen in this perspective, the prime fact about him
appeared that he had fallen in his encounter with Urizen and
come under his dominion, and the last was that his redemption
would be effected only by going down into self-annihilation and
death with Christ, and then rising again with the life of pure

imagination. Once imagination (Los) is supreme, then reason (Urizen) falls into his proper place, and the return into the eternal order is accomplished.

During Blake's stay at Felpham, Milton was continually present in the minds of both himself and Hayley. Hence he was for Blake an actual person in the Felpham drama, Mr and Mrs Blake and Hayley being with him the chief characters, and Skofield and his confederates the rabble. Then passing, as in *The French Revolution*, from actual persons and events to the unseen things of which they were the temporal manifestation, Blake saw each person in his eternal state, and as a symbol of that state, and he lost sight of the earthly puppets, as they were merged into their monstrous and eternal counterparts. The transition made, the poem is no longer intelligible to the corporeal understanding, and Hayley might read it a hundred times without suspecting that he was the villain of the piece.

The characters are Los, Urizen, Palamabron and Rintrah, sons of Los, Satan, and Skofield, who keeps his own name. Satan for a time is Hayley, Palamabron by turns Blake and Wesley, Rintrah, Whitefield. This is a seemingly harsh judgment of poor Hayley, akin to Michael Angelo's treatment of Biagio da Cesena ; but the harshness is humorously softened when Satan is discovered decked with half the graces. He is kind, meek, humble, and complains gently when his kindness fails to call forth gratitude. He is the personification of Hayley's virtues, which together make up (hypocritic) holiness.

Blake had made the startling discovery, which Nietzsche has popularized in our time, that the graces in wrong places are vices. Nietzsche went on to make the absurd assertions that humility and pity are the virtues of the herd and are never right in any place. Blake believed that the graces coupled with insight and understanding took on a new quality which made them divine.

To give examples : Blake, while submissive to Hayley, was humble, but at the risk of his birthright.

Hayley, exerting himself to find rich neighbours to sit for Blake to paint in miniature, was kind, but he was suffocating his genius.

To the scribes and Pharisees, Christ meek would have been Christ weak.

Modesty in one who does not know that all things that live are holy is prudery.

To pity oneself or another for the troubles that come through slackness is effeminacy. The true virtue here is to damn. Hence the right place for a man clothed from head to foot in hypocritic graces is hell, his right name is Satan.

But when a man has stripped himself of his virtues, and annihilating himself goes down with Christ into death, then he rises again into newness of life and vision, and the graces of the new life, still called by their old names, but now in their right places, are flaming, beautiful, irresistible.

Once Blake saw his man in his setting in eternity, he escaped from his initial resentment, and he could write calmly to Hayley and subscribe himself, "Your devoted Will Blake."

I may remark that Blake did not think he had invented new values, like Nietzsche, in his indictment of the virtues. His language was his own, but his conclusions were precisely the same as those of Wesley, Whitefield, Bunyan, St Paul, when they, in effect, speak of man's righteousness as filthy rags, and of his need to be clothed with the *living* righteousness of Christ before his garment can be reckoned beautiful and clean.

A few quotations from *Milton* may be given as Blake's final word on Hayley. I will write Hayley for Satan, and Blake for Palamabron.

" Blake, reddening like the Moon in an eclipse,
  Spoke, saying, You know Hayley's mildness and his self-imposition ;
  Seeming a brother, being a tyrant, even thinking himself a brother
  While he is murdering the just."

" How should Hayley know the duties of another ? "

" Hayley wept,
  And mildly cursing Blake, him accused of crimes himself had wrought."

" So Los said : Henceforth, Blake, let each his own station
  Keep ; nor in pity false, nor in officious brotherhood, where
  None needs be active."

" But Hayley, returning to his Mills (for Blake had served
  The Mills of Hayley as the easier task), found all confusion,
  And back returned to Los, not filled with vengeance, but with tears.
  Himself convinced of Blake's turpitude."

" Blake prayed :
  O God protect me from my friends."

" For Hayley, flaming with Rintrah's fury hidden beneath his own mildness,
  Accused Blake before the Assembly of ingratitude and malice."

" When Hayley, making to himself Laws from his own identity,
  Compelled others to serve him in moral gratitude and submission."

" Leutha said : ' Entering the doors of Hayley's brain night after night,
  Like sweet perfumes, I stupefied the masculine perceptions,
  And kept only the feminine awake ; hence rose his soft
  Delusory love to Blake.' "

" The Gnomes cursed
Hayley bitterly,
To do unkind thinks in kindness, with power armed ; to say
The most irritating things in the midst of tears and love—
These are the stings of the Serpent ! "

These are enough to show Blake's method, and his remorseless understanding of Hayley. There is present an irresistible touch of humour which preserves them from being too bitter.

For the rest, the poem narrates Milton's encounter with Urizen ; his going down into self-annihilation and death ; his judgment, and final redemption as he ascends to the heaven of the imagination. Milton's heaven is then the heaven of Jesus, and his hell remains its irreconcilable contrary.

In this poem Blake's full-grown mythology appears. The mythical persons, places, states are ominously present ; but since they appear with much more particularity in *The Four Zoas* and *Jerusalem*, I may pass to them to extract what is necessary for understanding the mature Blake.

Jerusalem and *The Four Zoas* should be studied together. The latter was begun about 1795, and rewritten at Felpham. The early prophetic books—*Urizen, Los*—stand as preliminary sketches to this large poem. They are woven into it with scarcely a change of word.

Blake's great scheme is mainly in line with historical Christianity, which of course is catholicism. He starts with the eternal order and unity. Without attempting to explain the origin of evil, he narrates the fall out of unity and order into diversity and disorder, and how as a consequence of the fall creation appears. He is obliged to use the word " creation," but there is no real creation in his cosmogony. There are only three possible theories of creation. Creation from within God, which is pantheism, and makes the universe an emanation ; creation from something outside of God, which is dualism, and not likely to be accepted in the West ; and creation out of nothing, which is catholicism. Blake learnt from Swedenborg the emanative theory. Swedenborg tried to avoid the pantheistic conclusion of his foundation principle, and believed that he had succeeded. His doctrine of the human God was certainly fine, and nearly catholic. Blake sways between the two. His doctrine of creation is pantheistic, but his affirmation that " God doth a human form display to those that dwell in realms of day " is splendidly catholic, and so, on the whole, is his doctrine of the fall. Since Blake's day the problem has become enormously complicated, because we have to take account of the vestiges in man's body of an animal ancestry, and the still more infallible signs in his soul of a divine origin. Perhaps we shall eventually all come to believe in both evolution and a special creation to account for man's unique place in the universe. At any rate a denial of the fall involves a definite departure from historical Christianity, and it is important to see that it was an integral part of Blake's scheme and without it that scheme falls to pieces. Not that he pressed the letter of the Adam and Eve story. It stood for him as a divinely simple witness of an ancient simplicity and unity from which man has departed by disobedience and the assertion of a life and a self independent of God. His way back into unity is by the cross of Jesus Christ, where the self-hood dies, and the day of judgment, which finally separates in him the gold from the dross, and presents him in his divine humanity perfect before the human-divine God.

Between these two stupendous facts—the fall and the redemption—Blake finds a place to say all that he wishes about the manifold things of heaven and earth and hell.

The unity from which man departs is made up of four mighty ones—the Four Zoas—who are the four beasts of the Apocalypse, taken from the four beasts of Ezekiel, who probably appropriated four of the many monstrous symbolical beasts of Assyria.

Blake invented names for them. Of these—Urizen, Urthona-Los, Luvah, and Tharmas—Urizen and Los are by far the clearest conceived figures. Perfect unity is maintained so long as Los is supreme. Reason is important in its right place. It becomes an evil when it usurps the place of imagination and thinks it can see as far. The essence of the fall is disorder. Redemption restores order, which is unity. Science alone breaks down because it is built up on observation and induction. Its observation is insufficient, for it is the observation of a shrunk universe. It gathers its materials through the five senses. But there are other avenues in regenerated man. If science were built up on the observation or vision of the whole instead of a very small part, it would become divine science and coincident with religion.

Religion breaks down whether built on nature or experience. If on nature, it is nature only as seen through limited vision; if on experience, it is the experience of fallen man, and therefore it is of vital force only when it transcends nature and becomes super-natural, and rests on a revelation not from man's experience, however deep, but from God.

Deism was the particular time-heresy of Blake's day. He came into direct contact with it through his friend Tom Paine.

ALBION.
From Jerusalem.

Deistic religion, to be adequate for man's need, must rest on perfect nature and perfect experience. Paine, Voltaire, and Rousseau, in order to provide these conditions which they saw to be necessary, were driven to make the wild statement, contrary to all experience, that man is naturally holy and good, and if he is not so as we know him, it is because he is everywhere perverted by artificial civilization. Having swallowed this baseless assumption, the rest was easy. They had only like Godwin to manufacture some scheme of political justice, or like Rousseau to arrange a social contract, and then the Millennium would come.

Against all this Blake protested, but without personal heat. He was well aware of Paine's deism, when he helped him to escape to France ; and of Voltaire he wrote justly : " He has sinned against the Son of man, and it shall be forgiven him." He protested and he affirmed : " Man is born a Spectre, or Satan, and is altogether an Evil." In this uncompromising affirmation, taken out of the heart of *Jerusalem*, written at the mature age of forty-seven, he cuts himself off sharply, not only from the humanitarian deism of his time, but from the pantheism that invaded so many phases of his thought ; he goes beyond the kindly catholic dogma which allows a residuum of original righteousness in fallen man ; and, with Whitefield and the Calvinists, denies that he has any righteousness left at all. Hence the utter failure of all empiricism, and the absolute need of Revelation and a supernatural religion. How near he was getting to Dr Johnson ! Super-nature, of course, presupposes nature. Blake was obliged to contemplate Nature, and meditate on the ancient difficulties that she still presents.

There are many passages in *The Four Zoas* to show how alive he was to Nature's loveliness and cruelty. Her cruelty

K

alone convinced him that she could not be taken as a basis for religion. A natural man building his character on a natural religion must be as cruel as his mother. The cruelty finds periodic vent in the lust of war.

Yet why there is so much cruelty in Nature remains a mystery, even to the man who has been driven by her to supernaturalism. Blake maintained that there were two ways of regarding Nature. The natural man, with only five senses to inform him, looks at her and sees a very small portion of the infinite, without ever suspecting the infinite. If he sees her loveliness it will arrest him and hold him fast. The spiritual man, on the contrary, looks not at but through Nature, to the spiritual world of which it is a vegetable mirror.

Here a difficulty presents itself. If Nature be a vegetable mirror of the eternal world, then her cruelties must reflect eternal cruelties. The spiritual man may see Nature far differently from the natural man, but that does not mean that she is merely the picture thrown by man's subjective self on the great abyss. If man were altogether exterminated her cruelties would still continue. Since Blake did not deny all existence to Nature, he was finally obliged to accept the old Christian explanation so finely summed up by St Paul in the eighth chapter of his Epistle to the Romans. Sin and disorder originate in the unseen heavens of the cosmos, where the principalities and powers dwell. Man repeats their sins, and Nature reflects the disorder of their cosmos. Hence there is no redemption in the cosmic heavens. Man enters on his redemption only when he bows the knee to Him who was raised above all heavens. And though " the whole creation groaneth and travaileth together until now," yet at the great manifestation of the sons of God she also " shall be delivered from the bondage of corruption into the glorious liberty of the children of God."

If the fall be denied, then the sufferings of nature and man must be referred to evolution, which taken alone solves something, but not the whole, of the ancient and baffling mystery.

All this explains finally why the great Memory to which Blake refers so often in *Jerusalem* cannot redeem a man. It is shut up in the cosmos. Memory would keep man in the cosmos even though he were reincarnated a million times. Memory's real work, whether for creative art or man's redemption, is in the fact that she gives man standing ground amid the horrors of infinity, until he takes strong hold of Him who overcame the world, and is lifted by Him into His ascension glory beyond the maddening whir of the cosmic wheels.

In these poems we get Blake's final attitude towards sex and passion.

Passion is always fire, and as such it is energy. To-day we are apt to use the word only for sex. In the eighteenth century passion was of any kind, and appetite stood for sex. With Blake, passion is man's vital worth. It may flame along many forbidden avenues, but once it has mounted to the imagination, and is controlled by spirit, then it is the driving force that makes man's works beautiful and his character spontaneous.

The passion of sex is, no doubt, the strongest of all. In the early prophetic books, when Blake was in a fever of rebellion, he affirmed that the sex passion was holy and should be free. Now in these later " prophecies " he still maintains, without wavering, the holiness of sex, but he no longer insists on free-love. He has no place for perversions. He steadily contemplates the normal impulse, and sees it as the principle of life impelling to love and children.

Each man has to solve his own sex problem. Blake's nature was exceptionally full and passionate. We caught a glimpse of him in his early married life panting in the whirlwind of sexual desire. It is probably true that he even contemplated following the patriarchal custom. But inconveniently for man's theories he has it brought home to him sooner or later that no man can live to himself alone. Mrs Blake had her feelings ; and though she was the most submissive and loyal of wives, yet she had the instinctive and normal objection to sharing her husband with others. Blake might argue that her objection was unreasonable, and that a truly unselfish woman should rise above such appropriation. But the stubborn fact remains that the woman who does so rise is either indifferent to her husband or abnormal, and Mrs. Blake, at any rate, both loving and unselfish to a heroic degree, was just here inflexible. King Solomon has sung the praises of a virtuous wife. We may take it as granted that her price is far above rubies. But the man who imperils his treasure by putting into practice some theory of free-love, however good that theory may seem in his own eyes, is worse than a fool ; and if he cannot endure some inconvenience for the sake of keeping the best gift that Heaven can bestow, he is unworthy to receive it.

Besides these facts, which must have forced their full attention on Blake as the years went by, time was modifying his early notions in other ways. He was an indefatigable worker. When one realizes the immense energy expended in creative work, and that Blake carried this on day after day, one sees that much of the sex energy must pass into another channel to supply the necessary power.

And lastly Blake's own spiritual life worked the change. As he learnt to see through Nature to her antetype, so he learnt to see through physical beauty. A beautiful face was a very transitory manifestation of eternal beauty. When Blake with Plato had pierced through to the unseen fount of beauty, then he was no longer a slave to externals. The passion remained, but transmuted, and legitimate relief was found in the continuous creation of beautiful things. Doubtless many will be disappointed that Blake's experience brought him back to traditional morality; but after all the terms on which he held it—a clean conception of sex, and faithfulness to a woman worthy of all faith—were not so very narrow and rigorous. They are terms that every man ought at once to accept, if ever he should be so fortunate as to have them proposed to him.

The above ideas are culled from *The Four Zoas* and *Jerusalem*. I do not propose any detailed analysis here. This I have done at some length in *Vision and Vesture*. I will merely point out in conclusion that although these poems seem to ramble all over the universe inside and outside without plan or order, there is, in fact, a connecting link in the figure of Albion.

Albion is the personification of the divine humanity ; but regarded individually he is fallen man, bound with " the pale limbs of his Eternal Individuality upon the Rock of Ages." His inward eyes are closed from the Divine Vision, and so he may be reckoned dead in trespasses and sin. Blake pronounced the natural man altogether an evil. But Albion is not an image of total depravity. Within him are all the divine faculties in addition to the five senses without, but they are closed. If he is to be redeemed, there is no need to create new spiritual faculties, but to re-create and make operative those that are already there. Hence Blake drives back of regeneration to the first generation, when man was made in the image and likeness of God. Regeneration is the renewal of the ancient image and likeness through the cross of Christ and the breath of the Divine Spirit.

Albion, like Lazarus, is sick. " He whom Thou lovest is sick. He wanders from his house of Eternity." His " exteriors are become indefinite, opened to pain, in a fierce, hungry void, and none can visit his regions."

Pained and impotent, he laments like Job :

" Oh I am nothing if I enter into judgment with Thee.
  If Thou withdraw Thy breath I die, and vanish into Hades ;
  If Thou dost lay Thy hand upon me, behold I am silent ;
  If Thou withhold Thy hand I perish like a leaf ;
  Oh I am nothing, and to nothing must return again.
  If Thou withdraw Thy breath, behold I am oblivion."

" Eternal death haunts all my expectations. Rent from Eternal Brotherhood we die and are no more."

And so Man like a corse

" lay on the Rock. The Sea of Time and Space
  Beat round the rocks in mighty waves."

Even his limbs " vegetated in monstrous forms of death."

He is opaque and contracted. Yet mercifully there is a limit to his opacity and contraction, named by Blake Satan and Adam ; else he would sleep eternally. The capacity remains to hear the Voice of the Son of God and live, and until tha moment he is guarded in tender care by the " mild and gentle " Saviour.

It is Heaven's purpose to awake him.

" Then all in great Eternity, which is called the Council of God,
Met as one Man, even Jesus—to awake the fallen Man.
The fallen Man stretched like a corse upon the oozy rock,
Washed with the tide, pale, overgrown with the waves,
Just moved with horrible dreams."

Albion like Milton must tread the difficult way of self-
annihilation and judgment.

His Day of Judgment is given with marvellous wealth of
detail in *The Four Zoas*, Night IX. But there are still finer
passages in *Jerusalem* which lead Albion to his final beatitude.

" Albion said : O Lord, what can I do ? my selfhood cruel
Marches against Thee . . .
I behold the visions of my deadly sleep of six thousand years,
Dazzling around Thy skirts like a serpent of precious stones and gold ;
I know it is my self, O my Divine Creator and Redeemer.

Jesus replied : Fear not, Albion ; unless I die thou canst not live,
But if I die I shall arise again and thou with Me.
This is Friendship and Brotherhood, without it Man Is Not.

Jesus said : Thus do Men in Eternity,
One for another, to put off by forgiveness every sin.

Albion replied : Cannot Man exist without mysterious
Offering of Self for Another ? is this Friendship and Brotherhood ?

Jesus said : Wouldest thou love one who never died
For thee, or ever die for one who had not died for thee ?
And if God dieth not for Man, and giveth not Himself
Eternally for Man, Man could not exist, for Man is Love
As God is Love ; every kindness to another is a little Death
In the Divine Image, nor can Man exist but by Brotherhood.

So saying, the Cloud overshadowing divided them asunder ;
Albion stood in terror, not for himself but for his Friend
Divine, and Self was lost in the contemplation of faith
And wonder at the Divine Mercy, and at Los's sublime honour."

Thus Blake leads man back into his ancient simplicity and unity. Order is restored ; and the four mighty ones that warred within to man's distraction, led captive by Los, are content each to perform his proper function, and so to prevent any further disturbance of the peace.

That is a fine consummation, but it is not Blake's last word. Perfect man must have a perfect City to dwell in. Albion redeemed must build Jerusalem. Blake began *Milton* with the fond contemplation of England's fields and meadows that he had loved in his youth. Calling for his weapons of war, he sang :

" I will not cease from Mental Fight,
    Nor shall my Sword sleep in my Hand,
    Till we have built Jerusalem
    In England's green and pleasant Land."

That vision may seem as far off as the vision of the prophet who declared, " The earth shall be filled with the knowledge of the Lord as the waters cover the sea." But the world's master-spirits have never been content that a man here and there should save his soul.

Plato imagined his Republic, Christ His Kingdom of God on earth, St John his Holy City, St Augustine his City of God. And Blake, whose first dreams had been in London's great city, still dreamed that man would return to his ancient simplicity, and build Jerusalem in England's green and pleasant land.

CHAPTER X

CROMEK, SIR JOSHUA, STOTHARD, AND CHAUCER

BLAKE had left Hayley to face poverty again in September 1803. He lodged at 17 South Molton Street, and from there he continued till December 11th, 1805, to write to the patron who had caused him so much inward disturbance. As long as he had thought it was possible to be on terms of complete friendship with Hayley he had quarrelled with him. Now he knew that such friendship was impossible. He saw Hayley as he was, and after years of self-conflict he saw himself as he was, and he recognized that there was no fundamental agreement to bridge over their differences. The effect of this discovery was to put him at peace with Hayley, and also to lower his sanguine expectations of a wide fellowship in this world.

The letters to Hayley are courteous and almost affectionate in tone. Hayley was occupied with his *Life of Romney*, Blake was hard at work on a *Head of Romney* and an engraving of the *Shipwreck*, after Romney. Hence there are many references to the artist from which we learn how genuine was Blake's admiration for the classic simplicity and the skilful massing of the lights and shades of Sir Joshua's great rival. Mr and Mrs Blake regularly send their love to Hayley and solicitations for his health till the correspondence gradually lessens, and Hayley, having no further use for Blake, gently closes it, and takes himself away out of his sight for ever. The severance was inevitable, and Blake could not be surprised. He jotted in his note-book :

"I write the rascal thanks till he and I
With thanks and compliments are both drawn dry."

And so the patron passes. The artist who has faced poverty is tasting its bitterness, stirred with the faint hope that he may find another patron who will be a corporeal friend and not a spiritual enemy. The patron in due time appeared. Robert Hartley Cromek was his name, print-jobber, book-maker, publisher, also an engraver who had studied under Bartolozzi.

This last fact was not auspicious. Blake, we know, had no regard for Bartolozzi's work, and a pupil of his might prove as little understanding of Blake's severe art as the Bard of Sussex. Still, there was hope. Cromek had an admirable business capacity. He understood how to advertise, to puff, to work the artist, and, what is still more materially important, to work the public. He had, in a word, all the practical qualities that Blake lacked. Blake with his love for uniting contraries believed that his art married to Cromek's practice might produce fame and money, and he was sorely in need of both.

At this time Blake was making designs for Blair's *Grave*, which he intended himself to engrave and publish. These were seen by Cromek, who admired them, and whose business instinct detected money in them. Immediately he proposed to publish a new edition of *The Grave*, and made a verbal agreement with Blake that he should contribute twelve engravings from his own designs. But, inspired by the same business instinct, it occurred to him that Blake's designs would sell much better if they were engraved by one who was known to be able to meet the popular taste. Accordingly he went off to Schiavonetti, who had been a fellow-pupil of Bartolozzi, and proposed to him to do the engravings.

The result was satisfactory to everyone except Blake. His illustrations appeared in the summer of 1808, and he received twenty guineas for his designs, but he was naturally furious and resentful against Cromek for playing him such a trick.

Cromek was quite right in his judgment that the Blake designs for *The Grave* would be popular. Yet this did not arise from any affinity between Blake and the then famous author of *The Grave*. Blair had been dead for fifty years. His poem expressed the strict orthodoxy of his day. Its fine passages are scarcely able to give vitality to the whole. Blake can have had no sympathy with the long-drawn-out description of the damask-cheeked maiden lying in her grave, the food of worms. The real genius of Christianity does not permit of such nauseous details of the charnel-house. We know how sensitive Blake was to the damask cheek of a maiden ; but we also know that he had come to regard it as the very transitory manifestation of the eternal beauty, and with his spiritual eye continually on the " Inviolable Rose " he did not need to remind himself of the mouldering relics in the grave.

He selected for what proved to be one of his finest designs Blair's description of the reunion of soul and body on the Day of Judgment. The poem repeats the doctrine of the resuscita-tion of the body that has long since returned to dust. Blake, of course, repudiated this dogma. He believed that the spiritual body is already present in one who has been born again of the spirit ; and, therefore, death is the bursting of the mortal shell that the spiritual body may pass on into its spiritual environment.

Yet with his love of marriages he depicted the rending of the tomb and the passionate reunion of soul and body, not because he believed in such a future event, but because that reunion taken symbolically was marvellously expressive of the rapturous marriage of many pairs of contraries that man in his day persisted in keeping apart.

For the rest, Blair's poem was sufficiently universal in its treatment of death to enable Blake to illustrate him, and yet read his own opinions into the words he selected.

Blake's indignation was hot against Cromek, as we can all understand. But unfortunately his soul was torn with the kindred passion of resentment, which he was inclined to nurse rather than exterminate. Here a little reason might have helped him ; but his distrust of reason, and his own passivity, led him to give vent to his resentments against successful men that strike us as captious and rude. He might plead the example of Christ in His treatment of the Pharisees, and he did jot down in his note-book words that I cannot help thinking he applied to himself:

> " Sir Joshua praises Michael Angelo.
> 'Tis Christian mildness when knaves praise a foe ;
> But 'twould be madness, all the world would say,
> Should Michael Angelo praise Sir Joshua—
> Christ used the Pharisees in a rougher way."

In answer to this we can but say that Sir Joshua was not a Pharisee, and that Blake was not Christ.

Blake's resentment against Sir Joshua seems to have begun at an interview when, a very young man, he had shown him some designs, and had been " recommended to work with less extravagance and more simplicity, and to correct his drawings." That was the sort of advice that he never would take at any time. One would have thought that if Sir Joshua was so palpably a Pharisee, Blake would not have troubled to ask his advice.

As the years passed, the significant facts about Sir Joshua and Blake were that the one was famous and rich, the other was unrecognized and poor. Blake's vision, sharpened just here by the injustice of fame, was preternaturally quick to discover that Sir Joshua was earthy and of the earth, while his own aim was the so much loftier one of piercing to the heavenly reality, and then expressing it by clear, definite, and " sweet outlines," and making the colours, lights, and shades serve to emphasize the heaven-revealing lines.

Sir Joshua died February 23rd, 1792. His coffin was carried to St Paul's followed by ninety coaches, and the most eloquent man of the day, Burke, was bidden to sing his praises. In 1808, when everyone was reading the collected *Discourses* of Reynolds, Blake too read, and as his custom was, made copious marginal notes. With the help of these we are able to relate Blake to Reynolds with a dispassionateness to which Blake could never attain.

What must strike any impartial reader of the *Discourses* is the extraordinary similarity of the aims of art there set forth with Blake's own cherished views. Both give the supreme place to Michael Angelo and extol Raphael. Both depreciate the Venetian and Flemish Schools. Both reckon good drawing the foundation of great art. The difference between them is mainly one of emphasis. Blake believed in impulse and instinct, and Sir Joshua in theoretical and reasoned deliberation. Yet the reasonable man writes : " If we were obliged to enter into a theoretical deliberation on every occasion, before we act, life would be at a stand, and art would be impracticable." And again : " I mean to caution you against . . . an unfounded distrust of the imagination and feeling in favour of narrow, partial, confined, argumentative theories." Both extol the grand style—with a difference. Reynolds's conception of the grand style is derived from the laborious study of the excellencies of many masters. When he attains to it, he is an epitome of those excellencies.

He reaches by this means his ideal, his heaven, and its contrary immediately bounds into view, which he is too urbane to call hell, and contents himself to designate as the real. Blake's ideal came to him with overmastering force from his direct vision of the inward reality. Hence he had no need of the false antithesis of the ideal and the real. Reynolds extols Michael Angelo and degrades Hogarth. Blake loves both. In conclusion we say, with only the *Discourses* [1] before us, the differences between the two men are negligible in a world where two men can never quite see eye to eye. It is when we turn from the *Discourses* to Sir Joshua's accomplished works that we begin to understand what was reasonable in Blake's furious resentment and attack.

Sir Joshua preached one thing and practised another. He sang the praises of the Florentine, Roman, and Bolognese Schools, and painted for all the world as if Rembrandt were his chief master.

> " Instead of ' Michael Angelo '
> Read ' Rembrandt,' for it is fit
> To make mere common honesty
> In all that he has writ."

Sir Joshua, after years of toil, painted Nelly O'Brien's petticoat, and we marvel at the consummate workmanship. Blake, in spite of his faulty technique and impatience of criticism, lifted

[1] Thirteenth Discourse.

the veil that hides the heavens, and inspires us. We thank those who make us wonder : we owe something deeper than thanks to those who inspire us. Blake was well aware that his art was of a loftier kind than that of the President of the Royal Academy. The one was reckoned the foremost painter of his age, the other was pitied as a madman. And Blake felt he did right to be angry.

Let us return to Cromek.

While Blake was at work on his designs for Blair's *Grave*, he drew a pencil sketch of *Chaucer's Canterbury Pilgrims*, which had always attracted him. Cromek, hopping in and out to see how the Blair designs were progressing, saw the sketch, and his brain immediately swarmed with fertile ideas. He proposed that Blake should engrave his design, and he would push it. But on second thoughts it occurred to him that the subject was admirably suited to Stothard's genius. Leaving Blake with nothing but a verbal agreement, he went straight off to Stothard, and proposed that he should make a design on the subject, for which he would pay him sixty guineas. Cromek undertook to find an engraver. Blake, who had been a friend of Stothard for many years, went to visit him, and found him at work on the *Canterbury Pilgrims*. Unsuspecting, he praised the work. Afterwards he discovered the part that Cromek had played in the seeming coincidence. At once he concluded that Stothard was privy to the deceit, and he included him in his vehement indignation against Cromek, and the lamb roared. With note-book at hand he jotted :

> " A petty sneaking knave I knew—
> O ! Mr. Cromek, how do ye do ? "

Stothard and Blake had been young together. It was he who had introduced him to Flaxman. The friendship, of course, was not of the closest, for they followed a very different track in art.

Flaxman and Blake had a common interest in Swedenborg as well as a supreme regard for outline, but Stothard's was always an outward eye, never inward. With a wife and many children, and everlastingly busy producing his thousands of designs, it was not to be expected that he should dive into inner causes. His contemporaries were content, and we too, that he should see the effects in a graceful and poetic glow, and reproduce them in soothing and graceful compositions. He peered into many times and many countries, but he was happier when illustrating his contemporaries, happiest when depicting the chequered career of Clarissa Harlowe.

Cromek was not wrong in thinking that Stothard would make a successful picture of the *Canterbury Pilgrims*. He was famous at grouping, had an eye for horses, and was willing to drudge at the British Museum to clothe his figures correctly. There was some difficulty about the engraving, which Cromek had first intended to entrust to Bromley. It passed successively through the hands of Lewis Schiavonetti, Engleheart, Niccolo Schiavonetti, and was finally done by James Heath. The result justified Cromek's calculations. The *Pilgrimage to Canterbury* was exhibited in all the great towns of England, and also in Edinburgh and Dublin. It had the most extensive sale of anything of the kind published within a hundred years. Everyone bought it and exhibited it, according to Mrs Bray, in their front parlour. It was reckoned Stothard's masterpiece. And when Harlow painted Stothard's portrait, he placed in the background a curtain just sufficiently drawn back to show the finest group of a picture in which the whole grouping was excellent.

Meanwhile Blake, determined to dispense with a professional advertiser, engraved his own design, and put it up for sale at 28 Broad Street, the house of his birth where his brother James carried on the business. But it was not to stand alone. It was exhibited together with sixteen historical inventions, eleven frescoes, seven drawings. Blake wrote a prospectus to the *Canterbury Pilgrims* and a *Descriptive Catalogue* to the whole collection. One or two people, notably Crabb Robinson, found their way to the room ; and while the praises of Stothard were being sung throughout the land for a design that had originated from Blake, Blake was tasting the bitter mortification of knowing that his attempt at self-advertisement and appeal to the public had failed.

Although comparisons are odious, we may give ourselves the luxury of comparing these two rival treatments of a fine subject.

Stothard's task was the easier of the two. His respect for and knowledge of Chaucer were much less than Blake's, and from the outset he had no mind to burden himself by attempting a servile copy of the poet. If the wife of Bath was just enjoying her fifth husband, then obviously she was no longer a pictorial subject, and Stothard took off as many years as the lady herself could have wished.

His treatment of the religious types was even less faithful. The protestantism of the eighteenth century regarded monks, friars, abbesses, and nuns merely as odd curiosities of an odd past. Stothard had religious feeling, as is evident in his picture *Confirmation*, which Landseer admired so much, but for him a friar was the type of laziness, and the monk of gluttony, and his only idea in portraying them was to

L

make the lines of their chins and stomachs as rotund as possible.

The idea of a pilgrimage was equally as remote from his mind. It was a foolishness to be pardoned only because it afforded the artist such excellent material for form and colour. But if Stothard had no wish to understand Chaucer's types and point of view, he was overjoyed at the chance of introducing so many horses, whose evolution from the Middle Ages was negligible. He had an eye for a horse, and could not resist the temptation of mounting his pilgrims on much finer horses than Chaucer provided, or they, for the most part, could afford. Finally he painted a pleasing background which Mrs Bray says was the Surrey Hills, and Blake the Dulwich Hills, but in either case were not passed by the Pilgrims in their journey from the Tabard. Inn to Canterbury.

The picture, as Hoppner said, is a modern one—charming, even captivating, and if it is not Chaucer, yet Stothard only took the liberty which Blake was ready to take himself when it suited his purpose.

Blake, for his part, was enormously attracted by Chaucer. He saw in him a first-rate example of the poetic genius that can pierce through to the underlying reality of every kind of man, and embrace him with genial warmth. He was observer and contemplator, and there was present just that element of imagination which always produces something original and creative.

The first happy result of Blake's capture by Chaucer was that he forgot for a time his horrid symbolism. When he illustrated his own poems, he drew his monstrous beasts without check, but now that there was no possibility of mounting Urizen and Los with the rest of the Pilgrims, he was driven to use Chaucer's symbolism, which time has proved to be universal.

Blake's sympathy here equals that of the elder poet. Like him he sees the fleshly weakness of the monks and friars, but he sees also, as Stothard could not, their strength and significance. The cook, the manciple, and the pardoner are low and coarse types affording the shade, but the parson, the knight, the squire, the abbess, the Oxford student, and the yeoman are bright types of human excellence that appear at all times, even in the eighteenth century, as Blake knew, though in a different dress.

The host on his good stout horse rightly holds the central place. The knight and squire lead the party as they ought. The religious types—monk, friar, abbess, nun, three priests—are grouped together. The most dignified figure is the parson— the person—seated on a wretched cob, for he cannot afford a better ; and near him, happy in his company, are the man of law and the yeoman. The wife of Bath, the miller, and the cook are different studies in sensuality. In the rear are the clerk of Oxenford and Chaucer himself, the philosopher and the poet, the poet being more prominent, since he with his poetic genius means more to us finally than the philosopher. Last of all comes the reeve, whose position accords with his office as steward.

Hence there is a spiritual significance in the picture. The pilgrims are real Chaucerian people on a real pilgrimage, grouped by a compelling spiritual kinship. The artist and poet are wedded. Yet the artist never loses his individuality, because the poet is so universal that he allows the artist to read his private experience into his own. The picture may not at first be so attractive as that of Stothard, but when one has grown accustomed to the exterior charms of the two pictures, there still remains in Blake's a rich field for fertile gleaning, while when the eye has become satiated with Stothard's sweetness there remains nothing else as food for the spirit.

CHAPTER XI

THE SUPREME VISION

BLAKE did well to be angry—so he believed. The years were slipping by, and the gleams of light that had promised a glad day now seldom came. Hayley had passed out of his life. Cromek could make the money out of him that he could not make for himself. Stothard, he believed, had acted with his eyes open. As he brooded on these things, anger and resentment took possession of him. His courage was failing. His resentments secreted poison that was surely spreading through his entire being and threatening to turn the once overtrustful Blake into a disillusioned and bitter old man.

Then he turned to the gospel, not like tens of thousands to find comfort, but to justify himself in his attitude of defiance, and to assure himself that his anger was godlike. He fixed his eyes on to the figure of Jesus, and essayed the difficult task of seeing Him as He was.

There was not much help coming even from those contemporaries whom he admired.

Wesley and Whitefield proclaimed incessantly the death of Jesus as the one availing sacrifice for sin, but they appeared to contemplate the life of Jesus as little as the great Apostle of the Gentiles. William Law, in a sweat of excitement at his finding of Boehme, devoted all his powers to discovering the riches of the mystical indwelling Christ.

Since Blake's day the higher critics have given their whole lives to carving out a human Jesus from the mass of myth, legend, and tradition. After this wholesale rejection of the supernatural, it strikes one as comic to hear Samuel Butler solemnly assuring us that there are many gaps in the character of Jesus that we may fill up, as we like, from our own ideals. The old dilemma was, Either Jesus was divine or He was not good : to-day it is, Either Jesus was falsely reported or He was mad.

To the old orthodoxy Jesus was all gentleness, meekness, and mildness. To the new heterodoxy He was afraid of reality and life, and in His manners vehement, impatient, and rude. Some see in Him the pattern of obedience : others the flaunter of all authority.

Blake, as we saw, had reckoned himself among the rebels. He pitted the future against the past. This was in his youth. Since then he had been learning that the past held endless treasures, and now he was forced to consider that it held Jesus. Rebellion must go beyond Jesus. Blake tried, but he could not pass Him. He gazed at Him until he was seized by Him. Passionately he contemplated Him. He perceived the energy and force of His anger and wrath, which like lightning struck the strongholds of evil and levelled them. He saw Him, His furious ire bursting forth until it became a chariot of fire. Then driving His course throughout the land, cursing the scribe and Pharisee, trampling down hypocrisy, breaking the Gates of Death till they let in day, with bright scourge in hand scourging the merchant Canaanite until :

> " With wrath He did subdue
> The serpent bulk of Nature's dross
> Till He had nailed it to the Cross."

THE PRAYER OF THE INFANT JESUS.
Reproduced by kind permission of Mr Sydney Morse.

Here was what Blake wanted—an anger and fury only greater than his own. He proceeded impatiently to tear to pieces the conventional Jesus.

Was Jesus obedient, or gentle, or humble? There is no simple answer. His life was dual—Godward and manward. To God He was obedient and humble : to man disobedient and proud. His life cannot be explained in terms of law, just because it was a life, and life is greater than law or logic. It was no more possible for Him to keep the letter of the ten commandments than for us. He set aside the Sabbath, He exposed His disciples to murder, He turned the law from harlots, He lived a vagrant life on other people's hard-won gains ; He coveted the best gifts for His friends ; He lived, not by laws and rules, but by an all-compelling instinct and impulse. He became in the eyes of His contemporaries a criminal only deserving of capital punishment.

Blake read on breathlessly.

A woman, a sinner taken in the act, was brought to this terrible Jesus. Instantly He became a lamb. With exquisite gentleness, sweetness, and tact, He spoke words chosen not to wound or shame her, and then sent her away forgiven and blest. This was no isolated event. His kindness to outcasts never failed. He was angry with Pharisees, yet even to them strangely without resentment. There was in Him a marvellously tender compassion, united with a hot hatred of meanness and hypocrisy. All fierce extremes met in Him. Here was what Blake had been seeking all his life—that for which he had been a rebel. Just here, in the old gospel, looming out of the past, he gained his supreme vision of One who satisfied his utmost need. He gazed, and worshipped Him in His immense energy and strength, His lowliness and meekness, Who had deserved all that His chosen people could give Him, yet had borne no resentment when they despised and rejected Him. Slowly Blake saw his life as a mere blot by the side of that resplendent life. Then all resentment died in him. The child spirit returned. He accepted his earthly lot, henceforth content to do his work with all his might, careless whether his generation paid the wages due to him or not.

CHAPTER XII

DECLINING YEARS AND DEATH

BLAKE, like the Patriarch, wrestled through his dark night till the day dawned. He had wrenched the secret out of the angel messenger. Henceforth he was an Israelite indeed—a guileless Prince with God, with a word of God on his lips for such as had ears to hear. Doubtless if we could arrange the details of human experience we would decree that after such a contact with the Divine a man should for the rest of his days sail on a halcyon sea into a haven of rest. But though the giants are slain, their ghosts return ; and Blake, like Jacob, was still haunted by spectres which only did not deter him because he had painfully learnt to discern between the shadow and the substance.

The day dawned, but not in the way that most would choose. Worldly success was farther from him than ever. Instead of himself arising like a blaze of light on the England that he loved, it was his spirit that was secretly illumined by the spiritual sun ; and while he could live by the memory of his resplendent vision of Christ, yet as he moved among men he was merely observed to halt on his thigh, or in other words to be touched with that frenzy or madness which marks those who have rashly gazed on the sun.

For the next ten years—years of rich spiritual maturity— Blake worked incessantly ; but his life was so obscure that his biographers have been able to glean but a handful of facts.

Immense changes were taking place in European literature and art. The new spirit and the old spirit were energetically at work side by side. At home, Jane Austen brought the novel as understood and treated by Fanny Burney to consummate perfection. Sir Walter Scott cast a magic glow of romance over the past. Wordsworth was piercing through the sacramental significance of nature. Coleridge was dreaming weird mystical dreams in the open daylight. Abroad, Goethe was exploring the riches of man's fallen nature. Beethoven, bursting away from Haydn, was introducing a world of passion into his music. Napoleon was a new kind of man.

Did Blake read the signs of the times ? And what did he think of them ? We know that he admired Wordsworth, but feared lest nature should ensnare him. The rest is guess-work. Blake could hardly have known how to place himself among the great moderns. It is we, looking back over the lapse of a century, who can see his deep affinity with many that came after him. I would say more. He had anticipated much of the better side of Nietzsche's teaching, but had seen it still more clearly in the character and teaching of Christ. He is strictly the Evangelist to the modern world enamoured of art, strength, and spontaneity, to bring it back to Christ.

Amidst these changes we can just discern a change in Blake's spiritual life which is common to all original geniuses. The Psalmist sang : " Instead of thy fathers thou shalt have children whom thou mayst make princes." Blake had hardly had a father, but he had had friends or brothers that were too apt to play the part of the heavy father. These were passing one by one, and their places were being taken by young men, sons who sat at the feet of the wise man and gave him the reverence that was his due.

We cannot say that Blake had a genius for friendship. With none of his old friends had he been really intimate. He was always uncompromising on his convictions, and these were so peculiar that not even Swedenborgian Flaxman could always understand him. His feeling for Flaxman survived with difficulty. What might have grown to a close friendship for Hayley died the moment he saw him as he was. Stothard had refused his offered hand after their quarrel. There remained Fuseli, of whom he wrote :

> "The only man that e'er I knew
> Who did not make me almost spew
> Was Fuseli."

Fuseli was a learned man who could scamper about the world's history with breathless speed. He lectured on the different ages of art with all the fluency of a Swiss polyglot waiter. Out of the copious flow of his eloquence one can, with long patience, fish up such fine things as this on Michael Angelo : " A beggar rose from his hand the patriarch of poverty," or this on Rembrandt's Crucifixion : " Rembrandt concentrated the tremendous moment in one flash of pallid light. It breaks on the body of Christ, shivers down His limbs, and vanishes on the armour of a crucifix ; the rest is gloom."

Fuseli had shared with Blake an admiration for Lavater. In an age of crude scepticism he openly confessed his faith in Christ. With Blake he reckoned outline the foundation of great art. Here was much on which the two men could meet. But Fuseli never quite dug down to fundamental principles.

He declared again and again that " our ideas are the offspring of our senses," and Blake regarded such damnable Lockian heresy

as rank atheism ; and among his other heresies, also damnable
in Blake's eyes, was an enthusiasm for Titian and Correggio,
and a summary denial that Albert Dürer was a man of genius.
Hence, Fuseli and Blake, with regard for one another, were never
intimate friends. It was about the year 1818 that Blake found
himself in the midst of a new and younger circle. George Cumberland, himself young and orthodox on outline, introduced him to
John Linnell and John Varley.

John Varley moved from 2 Harris Place to 5 Broad Street,
Golden Square, about 1806. His house was shared with William
Mulready, who married his sister. His wife, Esther, was sister
of John Gisborne, who moved in the Shelley and Godwin set.
Another sister married Copley Fielding. Here was a group of
artists connected by marriage.

Varley helped to found the Water Colour Society in 1804,
and drew to himself many young men who were more or less his
pupils. Among these, besides Mulready, were W. H. Hunt,
John Linnell, Samuel Palmer, James Holmes.

With the big, fat, genial Varley Blake soon became friends.
Varley was a typical once-born man, and his clean earthiness
made its irresistible appeal to the twice-born Blake with his head
in the skies. Besides his water-colours he pursued with equal
ardour and success the study of astrology.

Minds of Blake's order have been apt to believe in astrology,
like Jacob Boehme and Paracelsus ; but Varley failed to convert
Blake because, no doubt, of the extremely materialistic explanation that he could only give of his science. The stars, according
to the astrology that the Western mind scoffs at, are supposed
to exert a direct influence on the destinies and characters of men.
But there is an Oriental doctrine that dispenses with such a crude

theory, considering that the stars have no more direct influence on character than the hands of a clock on time. Like all mysticism, East and West, it regards the universe as the macrocosm and man the microcosm. Between the two there is a correspondence, and therefore the state of the microcosm can be read by the starry indications of the macrocosm as the time can be known by the hands of an exact clock or sundial.

Varley understood nothing of all this, and so failed to convince Blake. But he gave him what he needed far more, hearty good will and unpatronizing faith and reverence. Blake could pursue his visions and report on them, certain that his companion would believe in his marvels with that perfect credulity which so many are ready to give who have rejected the marvels of Christianity. At his bidding he evoked visions of past worthies, and sketched them while they waited. From 1819 to 1820 Blake executed no less than fifty heads, including his famous *Ghost of a Flea*.

Those of us who were thrilled in our boyhood by the tales of Lord Lytton like to know that Varley was consulted by him before writing his fascinating *Zanoni* and *Strange Story*.

A still greater comfort and help to Blake was John Linnell.

John Linnell began by copying George Morland, passed under the influence of Sir Benjamin West, and then became a pupil of Varley, who sent him straight to nature. Varley's brother Cornelius attended a baptist chapel, and he induced Linnell to go with him and listen to the sermons of its pastor, the Reverend John Martin. He was convicted of sin, converted, duly immersed, and regularly enrolled. Henceforth religion of a puritanic kind ruled his life, and made him easy to dissenters of the different sects, but stiff and uncompromising towards the Church of England and the clergy. At one time he had thoughts of joining the quakers, whose position is far different from that of the baptists; but he was deterred by Bernard Barton, who, though fond of art himself, warned him that the Friends as a whole looked with extreme suspicion on anyone addicted to such a questionable pursuit as that of making pictures.

Blake was introduced to Linnell by George Cumberland in 1818 at Linnell's house in Rathbone Place. They soon became intimate. Their religious conception of art united them, and Linnell much relished Blake's tirades against kings and priests. It was only when Blake spoke with equal licence of the sex passion that Linnell felt an adverse tug at their friendship.

Linnell took over for his country house Collins' Farm, North End, Hampstead, and there Blake became a regular visitor on Sunday afternoons until sickness and death put an end to his visits.

North End, now in the County of London, is still a village on the Heath. On Saturdays, Sundays, and Bank Holidays it is overlaid with trippers, orange-peel, and paper bags. But no sooner do the holiday-makers return to work than North End and its marvellous portion of heath resumes its mystery, and the dreamer can dream undisturbed till the next people's holiday.

It is pleasant to think of Blake arriving at Collins' Farm, then after the friendly greetings emerging by the Bull and Bush, sacred meeting-house of many artists, crossing the road to Rotten Row, mounting the hillock and viewing the fir-trees which still stand in all their mysterious beauty. If only North End had been south instead of north! Blake declared with seeming perverseness that the North upset his stomach. Varley would have explained to him that his ruling sign being Leo, he required like all lions the warm sunny south.

Linnell introduced him to many of his young friends, who, catching the infection, hailed Blake as a master and sat at his feet to learn. We note this deference because it is what Blake so richly deserved ; but even among his new young friends there was nothing like complete discipleship. Blake's art was an inseparable part of his whole passionate, chequered spiritual life. No one whose inner life does not repeat the same broad outlines can really approach near to him as an artist. James Holmes, with his easy, superficial, courtly life, might teach Blake to brighten his water-colours, but he was completely outside of his spiritual travail, and could only wonder mildly why young idealists like Calvert, Palmer, and Richmond could be so preoccupied with Blake's half-crazed thoughts.

Even among those chosen three, there were no sons of thunder.

Edward Calvert caught Blake's spirit in his lovely and simple woodcuts, but quite rightly followed his own bent, which led him ultimately along a different path from Blake's zigzag lightning tract. The master always transpierced Nature, and lived in a transcendental region : Calvert, serene and calm, detected the heart of the Divine beating equally in Nature, and reproduced what he heard and saw in musical and sweet landscapes, where storms never come, and which modern artists would probably prefer to see disturbed by an earthquake.

Samuel Palmer, with youthful impulse and generosity, gave himself to Blake, and, rendered receptive by his love and enthusiasm, soon assimilated all the master's principles. Palmer's rich nature allowed of much reverence for Linnell too, and in his early work it is easy to find examples first of Blake's influence and then of Linnell's. Like Calvert, he was deeply and equably devout. He did not demand that austerity which drew Linnell to the baptist, John Martin ; nor that passion for which Blake went to hell. The gentler elements of his soul led him away from harsh sects to the more temperate Church of England, which can, among other things, still nourish those souls that require the kind of diet that George Herbert could provide so bountifully.

We look with extreme interest to see how Blake's professed disciples set about to unite their religion and art. They did it as many other Christian artists have done it, as Fra Angelico did supremely well ; yet they missed Blake's dæmonic energy, and so have failed to meet that demand of our own age which will at all cost have passion for the driving force of religion if it is to have religion at all. Samuel Palmer painted and etched some exquisite pictures ; but he was in after years gently apologetic for Blake's *Marriage of Heaven and Hell*, and he left the problem of the synthesis of religion and art in the light of Christianity precisely where it was left by the best Italian Christian artists.

George Richmond completed the little inner circle of three disciples. He was only sixteen when he met Blake at John Linnell's, North End, and then walked with him back to Fountain Court, Strand, thrilling with a unique impression as if he were verily walking with the prophet Isaiah. For a while he was plastic clay in the hands of Blake, revealing the master's influence in *Abel the Shepherd* and *Christ and the Woman of Samaria*, but like his friends, Calvert and Palmer, he had sufficient native energy to follow his own instinct, and when he found himself in portrait painting there is nothing to remind us even remotely of Blake. His sitters appear a noble family. Cardinal Newman,

Bishop Wilberforce, Charlotte Brontë, Mrs Gaskell, and many others are extraordinarily beautiful, and might all be taken for brothers and sisters. Richmond's religious feelings brought him into fellowship with the tractarian movement, which of all recent religious movements in England allows most standing-ground for one devoted to religion and art. He did not paint Titans, but he puts us in love with his beautiful family, and that surely is no mean achievement.

Among Blake's friends must be mentioned Crabb Robinson and Frederick Tatham, not because of their intrinsic importance to Blake, but their use to us. Robinson was often sorely perplexed by the vehement paradoxes that Blake wilfully poured into his ears ; but at the same time, he thought it worth while to jot them down in his diary.

Tatham came near enough to Blake to enable him to fulfil several of the indispensable qualifications of the biographer. Afterwards he became an Irvingite, and, conscience-ridden, destroyed many of Blake's works that had come into his hands because he reckoned them unsound.

One other very curious friendship stands out, that with Thomas Griffiths Wainewright.

Wainewright was born out of due season. He might have avoided the unpleasant and ugly things that befell him if he had been a contemporary of the Borgias. He was an artist, and art is no respecter of persons. We are tempted to say that art is fallen man's supreme consolation. It is assuredly the meeting-place between a certain kind of saint and a certain kind of sinner. The highest artist-saint, like Jesus Christ, appears to create himself rather than works of art, and such always makes an irresistible appeal to the artist-sinner, as we see that Christ did to Oscar

M

Wilde in his *De Profundis* and to George Moore in his *Brook Kerith*. The latter seems to be as far as the artist can reach without religion, and it could teach most Christians something about their Master. When Blake discovered that the Real Man in each one of us has imagination for his chief and working faculty, he overcame once for all the provoking dualism of art and religion, and at the same time he became an attraction to those who live an imaginative life, especially among sinners. Wainewright was drawn to Blake for precisely the same reason that many modern enthusiasts are who could hardly be reckoned religious. He is permanently interesting to the psychologist as to the artist, and hence he could not escape the notice of Lord Lytton, who introduced him into his *Lucretia*, and above all of Oscar Wilde, who darted upon him, and who, with such a subject, was loosened to write in his most witty, brilliant, and characteristic style.

Here I must mention, in order, Blake's chief works from 1810 to the end.

In 1793 was published a small book of engravings *For Children, The Gates of Paradise*. Blake re-issued this in 1810, changing the *For Children* to *For the Sexes*. The changes do not throw fresh light on Blake. Rather, what is important to know, we see, in spite of the changes, that Blake's deepest thoughts were the same in 1795 and 1810. I will quote only the first two lines :

> " Mutual Forgiveness of each vice,
> Such are the Gates of Paradise."

Forgiveness of sins, so impossible for the Pharisee, so easy for the artist, is the heart of Christ's gospel. Blake leaned to that form of Christianity which best understood forgiveness. At this time he was inclined to think that the Church of Rome came nearest to Christ.

Blake reprinted *The Prologue and Characters of Chaucer's Pilgrims* in 1812. Then followed five years of indefatigable production, but the works are lost for this world, though Blake would probably say that they were published in the other, and read, and remembered.

About 1817 he engraved leaflets, *Laocoon*, and *On Homer's Poetry*, and *On Virgil*.

The first is covered with small writing, fresh proverbs of hell, which are the same in substance as the earlier proverbs, but less provocative. The *Laocoon* perfectly expressed his own experience during years of obscure struggle. He found the same mighty conflict described from cover to cover of the Bible. Christians have been accustomed to see there the history of their sin, conviction, struggle, and victory. Blake had nothing to say against all this, but he named that which was striving for the victory the spirit of art, and all the things that accompany the conflict—prayer, praise, fasting—he explained in terms of art. Protestantism had made necessary such a vehement vindication of the beautiful. To-day, I suppose, we accept naturally Blake's aphorisms, but need to rediscover some of those other things that protestantism and catholicism alike have insisted on so uncompromisingly in the past.

From *On Homer's Poetry* I quote the following :

" Unity and Morality are secondary considerations and belong to Philosophy and not to Poetry, to Exception and not to Rule, to Accident and not to Substance. The Ancients called it eating of the Tree of Good and Evil."

In other words, poetry, like life and love and other instinctive things, goes deeper and before our fine-spun distinctions of number and morality. Philosophers have sprung up since Blake's day who are wonderfully agreed with him.

This on the cause of European wars is striking : " The Classics ! it is the Classics, and not Goths nor Monks, that desolate Europe with Wars."

From *On Virgil* I gather this, which needs no comment : " A warlike State never can produce Art. It will rob and plunder and accumulate into one place, and translate and copy and buy and sell and criticize, but not make."

During Blake's last year in South Molton Street he executed seventeen woodcuts for Dr Thornton's *Pastorals of Virgil.* These are very simple and childlike or childish, according to our state when we look at Blake's work. They seem to me of very unequal merit ; but the best of them are invaluable, for they show that Blake at the age of sixty-three had not lost that childlike innocence, the parody of which is all that most men attain to in their second childhood.

In 1821 Blake removed to 3 Fountain Court, Strand, where he had the plainest of neutral rooms, not without value as a background for his visions. Here relief was at hand, but he knew it not. Harassed by poverty, he must raise money somehow. His collection of engravings, which had steadily grown since the day that he had endowed his bride with it as his sole treasure, was marketable, and with as little fuss as need be he sold it to Messrs Colnaghi and Company. It was the final self-stripping. Humbled and disciplined by the inexorable years, having surrendered himself and his last precious possession, he was ready to bring forth the rich fruit of his mature genius. His old friend and patron Butts gave him a commission to paint twenty-one water-colour designs illustrating the Book of Job. He was allowed to show them, and they drew forth from his friend Linnell a further commission to execute and engrave a duplicate set, with the written agreement that he should receive £100 for the designs and copyright and another £100 out of the profits. There were no profits forthcoming ; but Linnell paid him in instalments £50 besides the first £100. We may note here that the Royal Academy in 1822 made him a grant of £25. And so, at last, Blake had sufficient means to enable him to devote himself to his joyous work without the gnawing distraction of poverty and want.

There is no book in the world better suited for Blake's genius than the Book of Job. It has been in itself a complete Bible to the mystic in all ages. In it is given a marvellous description in dramatic form of that mysterious and awful self-stripping which the saint experiences after his conversion and not before. It is an expansion of the text that even here death is the gate of life. The same truth is insisted on by all the prophets, especially by the prophets to the nations like Ezekiel and Jonah; by the life, death, and resurrection of Jesus Christ ; by the personal experience of St Paul ; and recently by Hegel, till it has become a common-place both in religion and philosophy.

Blake was troubled by no modern criticism of the Book of Job, which by post-dating it several hundred years has robbed it of much of its literary interest. To him it was the porch of the Sanctuary, the oldest book in the Bible, at once the most ancient and most modern of books. Job, after his dark night of testing and judgment, emerged simple and guileless, a Patriarch who served God solely because that was the supremely right thing to do. Who was Job ? The Book gives no hint of his parentage. Who wrote the wonderful prologue ? Who could write it ? Again the Book is silent. Tradition says Moses ; and if tradition speak truly, then several very interesting things follow. Job was probably the son of Issachar,[1] and as such went down with his father into Egypt when Joseph had been advanced in that land. He would then remove to Uz in Chaldæa, carrying within treasures of Egyptian learning. In later years, Moses, fleeing from Egypt into the desert of Midian, would become his neighbour. Moses is admittedly one of the world's greatest initiates. As such he could certainly have written the prologue and the epilogue. And how lofty a level the drama maintains throughout ! Even Job's friends, who pour out pithy things in rich poetical language surpassing that attained by all laureates, are rebuked for uttering only what everybody knows. Yet so universal is the Book in its symbolism that it can afford, if need be, to dispense with picturesque details of its authorship and date, and stand simply on its merits as an inspired dramatic epic of Man's passage from his consciousness of degradation as a worm, and his stubbornness as a wild ass's colt, to the dignity and power of a son of God.

Blake had already traced the course of man's day of judgment in Night IX of *The Four Zoas*, and had painted a fresco of the subject in 1820. In the poem he had used his own peculiar mythology, and closed his poem to nearly all readers. The Book of Job obliged him to drop his own symbolism and use the simple and universal symbols that the drama itself supplies. A brief reference to each design in order will make his purpose clear.

[1] Genesis xlvi. 13.

Then went Satan forth from the presence of the Lord

Design I.—Job and his wife and family, like true Israelites, are at prayer under a spreading fig-tree. The shepherd sons have for the time left their flocks at rest and hanged their musical instruments on the tree. At first sight the picture presents a scene of idyllic peace. But there are ominous signs. The sun is setting, night is fast coming, and the fig-tree suggests the immemorial symbol of Israel's wrestling during the dark night.

Design II.—An illustration of the prologue of the Book. It is a marvellous representation of what an initiate only—a Moses, a Blake—could have imagined of the cosmos, with its heavenly portion peopled with the angelic sons of God in the middle, the earth and its inhabitants below, and above and beyond all God in His Heaven.

Satan, a magnificent figure, comes with the Sons of God to present himself before God. In his fiery aura are two shadowy figures making with him a trinity of evil.

Design III.—The crash of Job's family. He has built his house, and prospered regardless of those who made it possible for him to build it; and in the sudden turn of events it has become a mere ruin.

Design IV.—Job and his wife are under the fig-tree, the man bearing with noble and unbroken fortitude the arrival of bad news.

Design V.—Once more the cosmos. Satan is rushing headlong towards earth to wreak his full power on Job in the midst of his charities, yet forbidden to touch the one thing that Job would so gladly surrender, his life. Heaven cannot remain impassive at suffering on earth. Its sun is darkened and the Almighty on His Throne is grieved at His heart.

Design VI.—Satan's last malice on Job. He is reduced to sheer nakedness and wretchedness. Nothing of his former life that gave him comfort remains to him. He is " wrecked on God." " The Lord gave and the Lord hath taken away, Blessed be the name of the Lord." With such faith and resignation his sun has not quite set.

Design VII.—The friends arrive. Once more Blake felt at home from his personal experience. He had never had beyond Catherine and Robert a perfect spiritual friend. He had never lacked corporeal ones. The remembrance of them gave zest and spirit to the portrayal of Eliphaz the Temanite, Bildad the Shuhite, and Zophar the Naamathite.

Design VIII.—Job's corporeal friends have done their worst. They and his wife have quenched his last hope. His sun has gone down. Naked and covered with boils from the crown of his head to the sole of his foot, he lifts up both hands and curses the day that saw his birth.

Design IX.—The vision of Eliphaz, and his terror, for which Blake recalled his own terror on the threshold.

Design X.—The corporeal friends stripped of their wordy disguise. They are spiritual enemies that point the finger of scorn at the just, upright man. There is a glimmer of light on the horizon, for Job can still say, " Though He slay me, yet will I trust in Him."

Design XI.—A worse stage of misery. Hitherto Job had held fast his faith in God. Now he no longer sees God as He is. In the terrors of his dreams and visions he cannot discern between God and Satan. Satan stretches over him with a face reminiscent of God's. As Job turns away his head in horror, it becomes impossible for him to detect the cloven hoof ; and so he touches

Canst thou bind the sweet influences of Pleiades or loose the bands of Orion

Let there Be

Light

Let there be a

Firmament

Let the Waters be gathered together into one place

& let the Dry Land appear

And God made Two Great Lights

Sun

Moon

Let the Waters bring forth abundantly

Let the Earth bring forth

Cattle & Creeping thing & Beast

When the morning Stars sang together, & all the
Sons of God shouted for joy

W Blake

London, Published as the Act directs March 8. 1825 by W. Blake N 3 Fountain Court Strand.

that horror of great darkness, worse than all physical suffering, where not only man but God has turned His face, and in Its place loom the commandments of stone, which recall the darkness and thunders of Sinai.

Design XII.—The horror of darkness has passed. The stars are shining, and the youthful Elihu essays to utter the wisdom that the old men have lacked. Blake could recall the ministry of his young friends, who had come so recently into his life, and by their love had caused the stars to appear. Elihu does not utter perfect wisdom, for that cannot be reached from human experience.

Design XIII.—The source of perfect wisdom. " The Lord answered Job out of the Whirlwind." Job sees Him as He is in His true lineaments, and listens as the Almighty speaks. Blake, too, reads breathlessly the marvellous description of creation till his spirit flames up, and the creative fire gives birth to his next most glorious design.

Design XIV.—The creation and the immense joy of it. There is the creation of the whole cosmos, when the morning Stars sang together, and all the Sons of God shouted for joy. Never was such joy again till the beginning of the New Creation, when the Son of God was born in Bethlehem, as Luke, artist and saint, narrates with such artless simplicity and beauty. The Scriptures assure us of a time when that joy shall be eternal. Meanwhile it is the artists who in true creation have a foretaste of the joy. It is Blake who has presented it in its most spiritual and universal aspect.

Design XV.—A grotesque. I presume that Blake, like Leonardo da Vinci, discovered something grotesque as he explored the universe.

Design XVI.—The universe once more. It is the consummation of the judgment. Satan and his shadowy companions who dwell in man have taken definite form and substance. The man who has walked the way of excess has brought all his latent evil out, and has given it substance, so that he can arise in his strength and cast it out for ever.

Design XVII.—Job's beatific vision. He is blessed and his house, now only his wife, but through her and God's blessing he may be fruitful and multiply, and build his house in the divine order. His sun has risen and will no more set.

Design XVIII.—Job stands before an altar of burnt-offering. Like Jacob he has prevailed, and God accepts him and his prayers for his friends.

Design XIX.—Job and his wife once more under the fig-tree, whose fruit has ripened. He is the recipient of friendly gifts and offerings from his neighbours.

Design XX.—Job, with memories engraven on the chambers of his imagery, stretching forth his hands over his new family of beautiful daughters.

Design XXI.—A return to the first scene. But the sun is rising, and Job and his family, taking their instruments of art, are worshipping God in the beauty of holiness.

Blake completed his engravings for Job in March 1825, and they were published March 1826.

They might well have been the crowning work of his life, and followed by his *Nunc dimittis*, but there was boundless mental energy in the old man, though his body was failing.

FROM T IE DANTE SERIES.

It was in 1825 that Blake met Crabb Robinson at the house of Mr Aders, where Mrs Aders, daughter of Raphael Smith, was in the habit of entertaining many interesting people.

Crabb Robinson was a most excellent man—well accoutred, steady on his legs, with well-set head, without superstition, and just enough prejudice to starch his mind.

He knew Blake at the time that he was learning Italian for the sake of Dante that he might execute Dante designs for Linnell. From Robinson's reminiscences, we do just get a glimpse of Blake struggling with Dante, and delighting to mystify his respectable friend. Unfortunately, the reported references in their conversations to Dante are few, though enough perhaps to indicate Blake's attitude. He was not one of Dante's elect. But with closer study he was beginning to fall under his spell, and we may safely surmise that if Dante had come into Blake's life in his youth, instead of Swedenborg, Blake would have become the greatest catholic mystic artist of the age.

Little more remains to be told.

Blake in great pain of body—stomach trouble and shivering fits—was driven to his bed. When he knew the end was near, he said to his wife : " I have no grief but in leaving you, Catherine. We have lived happy, we have lived long, we have been ever together, but we shall be divided soon. Why should I fear death ? Nor do I fear it. I have endeavoured to live as Christ commanded, and I have sought to worship God truly in my own home, when I was not seen of men."

While the wife ministered to him he exclaimed suddenly, " You have ever been an angel to me, I will draw you." And he did. In answer to her, he expressed a wish to be buried at Bunhill Fields by the Church of England.

At midday on August 12th, 1827, he burst into strong joyous song, and then corrected his previous word about parting by assuring Catherine that he would always be there to take care of her.   Then he remained quite quiet till his spirit passed away.

EPILOGUE

Life is a voyage of discovery or rediscovery. Those, like Blake, born in a Christian land make the same voyage. The Christian tradition is handed on to us in our tender infancy, and most people take what their immediate teachers tell them, and live on that dry stock for the rest of their days. But the sinner and the genius, like Blake, early throw their inheritance overboard, and driven by native energy go in adventurous quest of new lands. The first half of Blake's life was spent thus. He would rebel at all costs, he would above all protest against what he hated—the religion of repression.

For many years Christianity and repression were for him synonymous terms. His craving was for expression. Parents, teachers, priests, kings, governments, were enemies to spontaneous self-expression. Then they must go. His youthful exuberance admitted of no half-measures. Like Ezekiel and Christ, he poured out his invective against hireling shepherds : unlike them, he ceased for a time to believe in good shepherds. One and all they were out to repress men's instincts and passions, until, driven in, the pent-up passion poisoned their whole nature, or in the weaker sort was rendered passive. Blake proclaimed his doctrine with vehemence, but no one regarded him.

Pursuing this course for many years, he perceived some wonderful things. Art is expression ; and he made an application of all the glories of art to human character. Teach men to express themselves, and then instead of their being as dull and similar as a flock of sheep governed by the herd instinct, they would grow into a beautiful variety. Man would create himself as an artist creates his works. The same law governed both. Repression when successful induced a nerveless, sapless type. Man became an overwhipped dog. Expression produced a strong, beautiful character above all petty and tiresome rules of conduct. The conduct of such is carelessly right.

It was by Blake's frank proclamation of the *ego* that he anticipated so much of what the modern apostles of the superman have made us all familiar with. From Ibsen's *Doll's House* to Nietzsche's *Thus spake Zarathustra*, confidence in the *ego* has been proclaimed as the means to liberty, beauty, and sovereignty ; and this has been accompanied by revivals on a large scale of those ancient mystery religions that turn on the culture of the divine *ego*.

This was a road of excess which Blake pursued as far as an individual might. In the nineteenth century the law of the *ego*, the struggle for life, the survival of the fittest, brute force, were regarded as all one, and transferred from the individual to the State, till in a few years the world was plunged into war.

Blake's voyage of rediscovery began during the Reign of Terror. The new teachers, like Swedenborg and Godwin, Tom Paine and Mary Wollstonecraft, failed to satisfy his own craving for expression. The Reign of Terror appalled him when it showed him his principle at work in the proletariat. Then it was that turning again to the Evangelists he made the wonderful discovery, which later apostles of the *ego* have not made, that Jesus Christ was the perfect example and embodiment of his vision. He had pictured to himself a man, impelled by a creative passion, whose character in every part should be manifestly the outcome of fiery energy. And there was the Man in the Subject of the Gospels. But he saw that Jesus Christ could not be labelled or classed. There was egoistic self-expression in Him, and there was self-renunciation. Somehow He had altogether escaped the modern dilemma of self-expression or self-sacrifice. Both were magnificently present in Him and united, because His self-expression was resting on His self-surrender to God. Give up God, and man swings perpetually between duty to neighbour and duty to self. Believe in and surrender to God, and each falls into its proper place. This was not the only synthesis in the character of Jesus. He was a union of all possible contraries. Gentleness and fierceness ; non-resistance and aggressive force ; non-resentment and fiery invective ; forgiveness and severe justice, haughty pride and lowliness ; self-confidence and utter dependence upon God, all were in Jesus. Henceforth Blake could keep his vision of Jesus and his vision of art, for they were one.

The next stage in rediscovery was to find out what the great body of dogmatic truth had affirmed about Jesus down the Christian centuries. Here he made little progress. He probably felt, as we all do at times, that the simplicity of the gospel was lost in the maze of dogmatic subtleties. The negative aspect of dogma, that it rules out all that would infringe on that simplicity, never occurred to him. His mind was governed and distracted by Hindoo pantheism, and catholic anthropomorphism filtered and diluted through Swedenborg. Even after he had repudiated Swedenborg the distraction remained. His new understanding of Christ taught him that he must accept the ultimate antinomy of good and evil, and that therefore Christ's heaven and hell must remain ; but the pantheism never abated its watery flood,

and the emphatic catholic teaching of transcendence and immanence gained no sufficient hold to deliver his mind.

The truth is that Blake was not a great thinker, still less a
system-builder. He ought to have found the best Christian
system while young and kept to it. Then he could have lived
his life of vision within coherent bounds. Clear, sharp dogma,
like outline in art, would have given rest to his mind, substance to his visions, and saved him from the waste of pour-
ing out a torrent of incoherent sayings containing scraps of
gnosticism, theosophy, rosicrucianism, and almost every heresy
under the sun.

The master-mind in his youth who could have given him a
sound system was Dr Johnson, and he would not listen to him.
How should the arch-rebel pay any attention to the arch-conser-
vator? Dr Johnson said many foolish things about things of
no great importance : he was wise in great matters. An ounce
of folly, like a dead fly in the ointment, suffices to put off the
fastidious rebel, who will seize hold of any excuse. Eventually
Blake subscribed to the same creed as Dr Johnson. That surely
is a marvellous unanimity for such diverse minds.

The master-mind in his age who could have given him a
better system than his own, and to whom he was beginning to
listen, was Dante. His catholicism may have been of a medieval
pattern, but it was very little infected with the time-spirit ; it is
even now finer than Swedenborg's fabrication, and modern
compared with the gnosticism that bulked so largely in Blake's
mind.

Blake makes no disciples, and no school can claim him,
but he speaks to all who have any mental equipment. His vision
of Christ, if we can make it our own and fill out its defects, will

put us beyond the modern worship of the superman, and take us out of that sectarianism which gains ascendancy for a little while because of its lightness and fragmentariness.

The confusion in Blake's mental life affects his art. He declared consistently in times of clear vision that outline, form, and foundation are the essence of spiritual things. This is beyond anything to be found in Sir Joshua's *Discourses*, and anticipates Benedetto Croce when he says that art is an ultimate, that " form is constant and is spiritual activity," while " matter is changeable," yet he accomplished many designs that Reynolds could have taught him to correct.

His later poems suffer still more. The energy in them is terrific, and they are filled with flashes of inspiration; but their atmosphere is murky, and never clears for more than fifty lines at a time. They are storehouses, but the one who would get anything out of them must bring his taper with him.

The early short poems, on the contrary, shine with their own light. *The Tiger* and *The Emmet* are written before his mind has time to plunge into the penumbra of his disorderly system.

Blake was still young in spirit when he died. One feels with him, as with Tolstoi, that he had far from come to the end of his tether. He was one of the few to whose years another threescore might have been added with advantage. Where would he have arrived ? I think when we remember that for more than twenty years before his death he was on the voyage of re-discovery, we may hazard the guess that he would have reached the catholic form of Christianity, having thrown overboard his private symbolism on the way ; and that then he would have produced great, long poems of crystalline clearness, which would have placed him by the side of the master-poets of the ages.

N

Yet it is idle work guessing at what might have been. We blame a man's times, or birth, or church, or what not for his failures, when we should look for some fundamental lack in his own equipment. That Blake was not quite one of our conquerors, then, we will not attribute to the eighteenth century or to Swedenborg's predominant influence in his early life, but simply to the fact that he lacked the strong, virile reason that could keep pace with the on-rush of his visions. He was all Los : Urizen, whom he repudiated with such scorn, alone could have balanced his nature and led him to the supreme achievement.

INDEX

Abel the Shepherd, 176
Abstract Philosophy, 109
Adam and Eve observed by Satan, 123
Aders, Mr and Mrs, 187
Age of Reason, 87, 93
Ahania, 111
Akashic Records, 132
Albion, 149–50
America: A Prophecy, 96–7, 98
American Independence, War of, 86, 87, 98
Ancient of Days, 101
Angelic Wisdom, 58
Angelico, Fra, 176
Arblay, M. d', 85
Asia, 109
Astrology, 172–3
Augustine, St, 152
Austen, Jane, 170

Barbauld, Mrs, 30
Bartolozzi, 17, 123, 154
Barton, Bernard, 174
Bas Bleu, 28
Basire, 17, 18
Bastille, the, 89, 90, 92
Bath, Lord, 29

Beaumont and Fletcher, 33
Beethoven, 170
Bible, the, 122, 133
Bildad, 184
Blair's *Grave*, 154–9
Blake, Catherine, 30, 31, 37, 38, 40, 66, 148
Blake, James (Sen.), 12, 39
Blake, James (Jun.), 39
Blake, Robert, 14, 39, 40, 45
Blake, William, born, 11 ; baptized, 12 ; vision at Peckham Rye, 13 ; books read, 14 ; learns drawing from Mr Pars, 15 ; apprenticed to Basire, 17 ; joins the Academy under Moser, 21 ; designs *Morning*, or *Glad Day*, 22 ; falls in love with Polly Wood, 23 ; marries Catherine Boucher, 24 ; meets Flaxman, 30 ; goes to Mrs Mathew's parties, 30 ; on war, 34–5 ; lodges at 23 Green Street, 37 ; moves to 27 Broad Street, 39 ; nurses Robert, 40 ; moves to 28 Poland Street, 40 ; engraves after Stothard, 44 ; Robert imparts method of engraving, 45 ; comments on Lavater's Aphorisms, 51 ; and Swedenborg,

55–80 ; reads and annotates *Angelic Wisdom*, 62–5 ; subscribes his name to tenets of the New Church, 66 ; on Swedenborg, 72 ; takes leave of Swedenborg, 80 ; among the rebels, 89 ; wears the *bonnet rouge*, 89 ; on sex, 94–6 ; moves to 13 Hercules Buildings, 98 ; engraves *Europe : A Prophecy*, 99, 101 ; illustrates Bürger's *Lenore*, 111 ; goes to Felpham, 117 ; paints miniatures, 119–21 ; learns Greek from Hayley, 121 ; returns to London, 127 ; South Molton Street, 127 ; vision clears after visit to Truchsess gallery, 129 ; and Sir J. Reynolds, 156–9 ; writes descriptive catalogue, 161 ; and Chaucer, 162–3 ; vision of Jesus Christ, 165–8 ; new friends, 172 ; and Varley, 172–3 ; removes to 3 Fountain Court, Strand, 180 ; sells his collection of engravings, 180 ; and Book of Job, 182–86 ; and Dante, 187 ; illness, 187 ; death, 188

Blue-stockings, the, 26–36

Boehme, Jacob, 23, 47, 49, 51, 56, 58, 72, 118, 165, 172

Bond Street, 21

Book for a Rainy Day, 30

Book of Ahania, 110

Book of Job, 181–2

Book of Los, 110

Book of Urizen, 106

Boucher, Catherine, 24

Bourdon, 129

Bousset, 61

Boydell's Shakespeare Gallery, 123

Brahma, 109

Bray, Mrs, 160, 162

Breughel, 129

Brontë, Charlotte, 177

Brook Kerith, 178

Brooke, Mrs, 30

Bull and Bush, North End, Hampstead, 174

Bunyan, John, 140

Bürger, 111, 112

Burke, Edmund, 85, 89

Burney, Dr, 29

Burney, Fanny, 28, 42, 85, 86, 170

Butler, Samuel, 166

Butts, Thomas, 121, 124, 125, 127, 132

Calvert, Edward, 175, 176

Candide, 28

Caracci, 126

Carter, Mrs, 26, 27, 28, 30

Castle of Otranto, 34

Catherine of Siena, St, 53, 133

Chapone, Mrs, 30, 31

Chatterton, 14

Chaucer, 161, 162, 163

Chaucer's *Canterbury Pilgrims*, 159

Chesterfield, Lord, *Letters to his Son*, 27

Christ, 152

Christ and the Woman of Samaria, 176

Clod, the, 104

Coleridge, S. T., 82, 170

Collins' Farm, North End, Hampstead, 174

Correggio, 126, 172
Cosmos, the, 134, 147, 183, 185
Cowper, W., 82, 116, 123, 124, 130
Cowper, Life of, 130
Crime and Punishment, 98
Croce, Benedetto, 193
Cromek, Robert Hartley, 154–6, 159, 160, 165
Cumberland, George, 172

Dante, 73, 114, 133, 187, 192
Deism, 144–5
De Profundis, 178
Designs for Job, 183–6
Dialogues of the Dead, 26
Dogma, 192
Dostoieffski, 98
Dualism, 143
Dürer, Albert, 16, 17, 41, 42, 129, 172

Earl Godwin, 42
Ego-theism, 71
Elihu, 185
Elinor, 112
Eliot, George, 112
Eliphaz, 184
Elizabethan age, 16
Emmet, the, 193
Engleheart, 160
Enitharmon, 99, 100, 108
Eno, 111
Enquiry concerning Political Justice, 82
Epipsychidion, 95
Essay on Old Maids, 121
Essenes, the, 61

Europe, 109
Europe : A Prophecy, 99–101
Evelina, 42
Ezekiel, 137, 144, 181, 189
Ezra, 118

Fair Elinor, 34
Felpham, 117, 119, 125, 126
Fénelon, 50, 53
Fielding, Copley, 172
Fingal, 14
Flaxman, 22, 24, 25, 29, 30, 31, 116, 117, 118, 119, 121, 123, 159, 160, 171
Flaxman, Maria, 114
Flemish *picturesque,* 125
Florentine School of Art, 16
Fludd, 23
Foote, Samuel, 49
Fordyce, Dr, 85
France, 109
Francis of Assisi, St, 45
Franklin, 96
French Revolution, 85, 87, 89, 90–2, 101, 118
Fuseli, 24, 81, 171–2
Fuzon, 110, 111

Garrick, 115
Gaskell, Mrs, 177
Gates of Paradise, 178
Genlis, Madame de, 86
Ghost of a Flea, 173
Gibbon, Edward, 115
Gilchrist, 45
Glad Day, 42

Gnosticism, 134
Godwin, W., 82-4, 86, 87, 88, 92, 145, 172, 190
Goethe, 30, 36, 54, 170
Goldsmith, Oliver, 18
Gordon, Lord George, 23
Gothic architecture, 17
Grand Style, 125
Gregory, Dr, 85
Guyon, Madame, 23, 47, 50
Gwen, King of Norway, 34

Habakkuk, 129
Halls of Los, 122
Hamilton, 42
Hardy, 88
Harlow, 160
Haydn, 170
Hayley, William, 114-130, 137, 139-42, 153-4, 165, 171
Head of Romney, 153
Heath, James, 160
Heaven and Hell, 78
Hegel, 181
Hell, 57
Hemskerck, Martin, 16
Herbert, George, 176
Hervey, 49, 50
Hesketh, Lady, 116
Highland Society, 14
Hogarth, 42, 43, 158
Holbein, Hans, 129
Holcroft, 88
Holmes, James, 172, 175
Hoppner, 162
How sweet I roam'd, 16, 33

Hume, 36
Hunt, W. H., 172

Ibsen, 190
Imagination, 122, 125
Imlay, Charles, 86
Immanence, 192
Inspiration, 122, 132, 133
Isaiah, 118

Jacob, 169
Jefferson, 87
Jerusalem, 113, 131, 132, 142, 149, 151
Jesus Christ, 165-8, 189, 190-1
Job, Book of, 76
John, Saint, 152
Johnson, bookseller, 22, 81, 82, 86, 90, 123
Johnson, Dr, 20, 27, 28, 36, 47, 48, 145, 192
Johnson, Rev. John, 119, 122
Jonah, 181
Jonson, Ben, 14, 16, 31, 33
Joseph of Arimathea, 18
Juniper Hall, 85

Kaufmann, Angelica, 17
Keim, 61
King Edward the Third, 33
King Edward and Queen Elinor, 42
Klopstock's *Messiah*, 122

Landseer, 161
Laocoon, 179
Lavater, 50-4, 171
Law, William, 48, 165

Le Brun, 21
Lenore, Bürger's, 111
Linnell, John, 172, 173–5, 181
Little Girl Found, 103
Little Girl Lost, 103
Little Tom the Sailor, 119
Locke, John, 109
London, Bishop of, 29
Los, 75, 107, 108, 109, 139, 144, 194
Luke, St, 185
Luvah, 144
Lyca, 104
Lyttelton, Lord, 26, 29
Lytton, Bulwer, 82, 173, 178

Mackintosh, 89
Macpherson, 14, 15, 42
Mad Song, 33
Maimonides, 54
Marriage of Heaven and Hell, 75, 81, 176
Martin, Rev. John, 173, 176
Mathew, Mrs, 25, 29, 30, 31, 32, 35, 39, 44, 119
Mathew, Rev. Henry, 29, 30, 32
Memory, 122, 132, 133, 135, 136, 137, 147
Mendelssohn, Moses, 54
Meyer, 115
Michael Angelo, 16, 17, 18, 21, 42, 44, 117, 126, 129, 139, 157, 158, 171
Milton, John, 44, 76, 105, 118, 123–4, 132, 133, 137, 138, 139, 151
Milton, 122, 124, 131, 132, 137–142, 152
Miniature Painting, 119, 120, 121, 125
Montagu, Mrs, 26, 27, 28, 29, 30, 35

Moore, George, 61, 178
More, Hannah, 28, 115
Morland, George, 173
Morning, or *Glad Day*, 22
Morris, Mr, 71
Mortimer, 42
Moses, 182, 183
Mulgrave, Lord, 29
Mulready, W., 172
Muses, the, 122
My Silks and Fine Array, 33
Mysterious Mother, 34
Mysticism, German, 68

Napoleon, 170
Narbonne, M. de, 85
Nature, 13, 125, 146, 149
Nelly O'Brien, 158
Newman, Cardinal, 176
Newton, Sir Isaac, 109
Nietzsche, 54, 133, 139, 140, 170, 190
Night Thoughts, Young's, 112
No Popery Riots, 23
North American States, 44
North End, Hampstead, 174, 176

Odin, 109
On Homer's Poetry, 179
On Virgil, 179, 180
Oothoon, 94–5
Opie, Mrs, 115
Oram, 30
Orc, 99, 100, 109, 110
Ord, Mrs, 28
Ossian, 14
Ossian, 105

Paine, Tom, 82, 86–8, 89, 93, 96, 98, 144, 145, 190
Palamabron, 109
Palmer, Samuel, 172, 175–6
Pantheism, 71, 72, 106, 107, 143
Pantheism, Hindoo, 191
Paracelsus, 23, 47, 58, 118, 172
Paradise Lost, 136
Parker, 39, 40
Pars, Mr, 15
Pascal, 28
Passion, 76, 77, 147–8
Pastorals of Virgil, 180
Paul, St, 134, 135, 140, 146, 181
Paulus, Dr, 61
Pebble, the, 154
Penance of Jane Shore, 42
Pepys, Sir Lucas, 29
Percy's *Reliques*, 14
Phillips, Captain, 29
Pilgrimage to Canterbury, 160–1
Piozzi, Mrs, 84
Plato, 109, 149, 152
Poetical Sketches, 33, 44
Poison Tree, 104
Pope, A., 114
Portland, Duchess of, 26
Price, Dr, 82
Priestley, Dr, 82, 87, 93
Proverbs of Hell, 76
Pythagoras, 109

Quakers, 174
Quintilian, 28

Radcliffe, Mrs, 34

Raphael, 16, 21, 42, 126, 157
Reign of Terror, 89, 100, 102, 117, 190
Rembrandt, 42, 158, 171
Renan, 61
Repression, 189–90, 191
Reynolds, Sir Joshua, 118, 126, 156–9, 193
Reynolds' *Discourses*, 157–8, 193
Richmond, George, 176–7
Rights of Man, 88
Rintrah, 109
Ritson's *English Songs*, 44
Robinson, Crabb, 161, 177, 187
Romano, Julio, 16
Romney, 115, 116, 118, 119, 123, 124, 130
Romney, Life of, 130
Rose, Samuel, 127
Rotten Row, Hampstead, 174
Rousseau, 28, 36, 109, 145
Rowley, 14
Royal Academy, 21, 25
Rubens, 21, 42

Samson, Dr, 99
Satan, 76, 139, 183, 184, 186
Schiavonetti, Lewis, 155, 160
Schiavonetti, Niccolo, 160
Schoolboy, the, 104
Schweitzer, 61
Scott, Sir W., 14, 170
Seven Planes, 134
Seward, Anna, 115
Sex, 147–8
Shakespeare, 14, 26, 27, 33, 44, 76, 118, 132, 133

Sharpe, 123
Shelley, 71, 84, 95, 133, 172
Shields, F., 112
Shipwreck, after Romney, 130, 153
Skofield, 127
Smelt, Mr, 29
Smith, J. T., 30, 39
Socrates, 109
Song of Liberty, 93
Song of Los, 108
Songs of Experience, 70
Songs of Innocence, 69, 102, 103
Sotho, 109
Spencer, 31
Spencer's *Faery Queen*, 14
Staël, Madame de, 86
Stothard, 22, 24, 44, 112, 114, 159, 160, 161, 162, 164, 165, 171
Strange Story, 173
Strauss, 61
Swedenborg, 30, 39, 49, 51, 52, 53, 55–80, 58, 59, 105, 110, 118, 137, 138, 143, 160, 187, 190, 191, 192, 194
Swinburne, 14, 33, 53
Symbolism, 136

Tabard Inn, 162
Talleyrand, 85
Tatham, F., 177
Tharmas, 144
The Divine Image, 69
The Little Vagabond, 71
Thel, 66–9
Thelwall, 86

Theosophy, 134
Theotormon, 94–5
Theresa, St, 23, 47, 50
Thomson, 14
Thornton, Dr, 180
Thus Spake Zarathustra, 190
Tiger, the, 193
Tiriel, 66, 67
Titian, 42, 172
Tolstoï, 193
Tooke, Horne, 86
Townshend, Charles, 87
Transcendence, 192
Trismegistus, 109
Triumphs of Temper, 114, 115, 121
Truchsess, Count, 129

Urizen, 66, 67, 75, 93, 99, 106, 107, 108, 110, 111, 139, 142, 144, 194

Varley, Cornelius, 173
Varley, John, 172–3, 174
Venetian art, 117
Venetian *finesse*, 125
Vesey, Mrs, 28
Vinci, Leonardo da, 129, 185
Visions of the Daughters of Albion, 94–5, 97
Voltaire, 28, 36, 109, 145

Wainewright, T. G., 177–8
Walpole, Horace, 26, 28, 34, 85
War, 34, 35, 43, 44
Warren, 96
Washington, 96

O

Water Colour Society, 172
Watson, Caroline, 130
Watteau, 129
Webster, 33
Werther, 28
Wesley, John, 23, 48, 49, 50, 66, 139, 140, 165
West, Sir Benjamin, 173
Whitefield, 23, 49, 50, 66, 139, 140, 145, 165
Wilberforce, 177
Wilde, Oscar, 178
Wilkinson, Garth, 53, 68, 71, 72

Wollstonecraft, Mary, 82, 84–6, 88, 89, 92, 190
Wood, Polly, 23
Woollett, 17, 18
Wordsworth, 13, 170

Yeats, W. B., 112, 132
Young, Edward, 112

Zanoni, 173
Zoas, the Four, 113, 131, 124, 142, 145, 182
Zophar, 184